LEADERSHIP FROM BELOW

Trond Arne Undheim, PhD

Leadership from Below

Copyright © 2009 by Trond Arne Undheim

ISBN 978-1-4357-1122-8

Second Edition

www.leadershipfrombelow.com

Endorsements

A must-read for any young manager looking to apply the lessons of eBay, Google and Facebook to the real world. Too often, talented executives are limited by the bureaucratic and political realities of life in a big corporation. This book closes the gap between the freedoms and possibilities of the wired world and the day to day burdens of the cubicle, and as such it is an indispensable tool.
Julian Herbstein, Partner, BFDM, formerly Principal with Soros Fund Management.

"I normally do not care much for management books. This one is different. This is not a book for wannabe executives, although they might benefit too. Rather, it is a book containing real strategies for real people, based on a philosophy of leadership and a way of thinking that at first seems so obvious, yet at the same time remains so elusive to most of us. It may not teach you how to become a millionaire in six months. It may however genuinely help you become a more effective you."
Espen Moe, Ph.D, Author of Governance, Growth and Global Leadership, Ashgate, 2007.

"Just like Covey's Seven habits of highly effective people, this is a must read. It teaches that everyone can be a leader irrespective of their place in the hierarchy. Key is to rethink all aspects of the immediate surroundings in your office: your place in the corporate culture, your boss, your equipment, and the time you spend there (and not at home!). Trond Undheim's insight based on his wide experience combined with universal wisdom shows how to capitalize on your daily struggles and how to become empowered. 'Leadership from Below' can be regarded as the toolkit to grow with the right attitude.
Freek Van Krevel, National Expert e-government, European Commission.

To my daughter, the very best teacher of leadership from below.

LEADERSHIP FROM BELOW

Trond Arne Undheim, PhD

Contents

*P*reface

A new generation of leaders is being bred, but the management literature has not caught on. Leaders need a new bible. Management is about doing things right. Leadership is about doing the right things. Both are about to change radically. The trends are already there: They herald an age of leadership from below – an apparent oxymoron. In the future, effective leadership will have nothing to do with hierarchy and formal position. Rather, it will be project based. Those who excel at being aware, sharing, and pooling knowledge, win.

Leadership from below originates in Scandinavia with work-life balance, peer leadership, coaching, mentoring, and interdisciplinary teamwork. Project-based approaches like self-governed groups were pioneered in Scandinavian companies like Volvo in the 1980s. Linus Torvalds of Finland, who developed the Linux operating system, has inspired a growing use of Open Source principles across the globe. There are also European influences. The World Wide Web was developed by Englishman Tim Berners-Lee at the Swiss particle physics lab at CERN. Other influences originate in Asia, like the principles of ba, Zen, feng shui, kanso, and ki, the importance of which I will explain in the coming pages. Finally, multicultural diversity and technological dependence are global trends that demand constant attention.

The emerging lifestyle of the global knowledge worker can take a toll on human relationships. This book offers practical, intellectual, and spiritual guidance.

There are books that talk about how to deal with the impact of Generation Y – those born between 1970 and 1990. This book, in contrast, is written from that generation's perspective, which is entirely different. Whether you are a manager, a C-level executive, or a public servant, this book will sting like a bee.

Brussels, 16 February 2008
Trond Arne Undheim

$\mathcal{P}$reface to the Paperback Edition

While this paperback edition is not an updated text, I wanted to point out that I have had testimony from many readers who agree with the main argument, based on their own experience. This is encouraging!

London, 9 January 2009,
Trond Arne Undheim

*I*ntroduction

Leadership from below means looking beyond the hierarchy. In other words, you can be a leader even if you do not yet have a managerial position. A good leader knows when to lead and when to let others lead; wherever she ranks, she knows how to deal with networks and hierarchies – from above or below.

*T*oday's work practices are rapidly changing. Networks seem to matter more than teams, jobs, or employers. People spend less time in their offices. Some do not even have offices. Workers move around. Opportunities arise from technology, mobility, and globalization. Yet obstacles such as time, resources, and competition prevail. You also need to gain access. Face-to-face communication continues to matter. As new conditions emerge, and some prevail, individuals and teams must adapt. Being present means engaging in leadership from below: know how to show presence -- online and offline.

You may want to know why I have coined the phrase "leadership from below". After all, isn't that a contradiction in terms? Doesn't leadership have to do with management and with the qualities displayed by people at the top?

Since Peter F. Drucker popularized the field of management in the 1950s, no criticism to him intended, the field has become mostly about leadership at the top or formal leadership -- not about teamwork or accidental leadership. Hundreds of thousands of books have been written on management (i.e., how to lead workers successfully if you are put in charge). The problem is that most people are not in charge. And even when they are in charge, they are vastly outnumbered by those who are not. However, nobody is ever in charge of everything (on this earth, anyway). You do not control your competitors, your spouse, your kids, or your neighbors. A decade ago, there was a large power distance[1] between leader and disciple or when leaders divided tasks based on self-evident skills. People spent their whole lives in one organization, with defined hierarchies and set rules for how to move up the ladder. Management was dictated by experience. Respect was given, not earned.

Today's workplace is different. People move around. They often possess skills more advanced than their managers. Everyone reading this book has been in that position: knowing more than the boss (who usually knows more than his boss). Then the question becomes, "How do you handle that?" Do you try to manage your boss, as some management books preach these days? Being told to take charge is often a curse. Being in charge is not.

Life has many unknowns, professional life, too. What can successful individuals do to build a meaningful career today? How do you successfully work in a team? How do you build connections? How can you keep up with technology?

I have found that presence is the key to success: be there for other people; be present in your own life. Our sometimes rushed, nomadic lives are filled with technologies that make absence possible, even preferable. In contrast, why not master your surroundings by actually *being there*?

Technology should enhance communication, not become what we talk about. The time spent talking about new cell phone models -- or fiddling with them -- is time away from both work and play. We need to stop foreign objects from having an impact our daily life.

When I realized my cell phone was taking charge of my life, I quit. I lived without for two full years, from 2004 to 2006, and I seldom missed it. Now, slowly, it is becoming a part of my life again -- first as a "Batphone" within the family, and now for close friends and occasionally for colleagues. But I am keeping close guard. I have rules now: never pick up during meals, never after 8 pm. Only my boss and my wife overrule this approach. Dependency is never far away. The telephone interrupts meals, conversations, and sleep -- even in silent mode. While not disruptive to others, when you can feel your cell phone vibrating in your pocket, you feel compelled to answer. E-mail is easier to momentarily ignore, since its textual narrative is both less imposing and less immediate than the oral. Even email can become addictive; in a work context, you cannot ignore it for long. Instant messaging, of course, comes back and hits you in the head – text you cannot ignore. While instant communications offer multifarious opportunities for increased efficiency and efficacy, they can become a burden. Regardless of media, it would be best to set limits for its use and follow through. Intel co-founder Andy Grove said, "Only the paranoid survive." However, the opposite may be true, since only the balanced leaders survive (and have families, work-life balance, hobbies, and friends).

In fact, technologies have politics -- the politics of its designers.[2] The product designer's choices -- flat screens, fancy colors, small buttons -- are what you and I end up taking for granted. Instead, we should remain in control.

Not that we advocate absolute Luddism – anti-technology manifestos are counterproductive. Leaders must know technology – at least enough to take a strategic perspective. The right question to ask is: What do we need? Then, find the right solution, which may or may not include technology.

Let us imagine the year 2005 in the immediate aftermath of Hurricane Katrina.[3] There is massive devastation of New Orleans. Neither the mayor nor the governor is in control. The Federal Emergency Management Agency (FEMA) is not immediately mobilized. The president does not act with force immediately. Chris, a friend of ours, volunteers, among many, and suddenly finds himself in charge of a large part of the rescue operation for a few days. Lucky for him and for New Orleans, he has a logistics background from the United States Military Academy at West Point. Although, in retrospect, the power vacuum is shocking, what counted for the people on the ground was that there was a leader on the ground. Nothing else mattered.

In an ideal world, respect should be conferred independent of formal position in a hierarchy. However, people may envy a young leader and try to give him or her a hard time. Performing leadership from below is to be cognizant of the advanced power plays, but not paralyzed by them. Not to care too much. Action counts more than words.

Think like a teacher. When I give a speech, I say to myself, the only difference between my audience and me is preparation. Never treat people as if you have any other advantage. From experience, many traditional authority figures do not think that way. The trouble for them is that we are starting to notice.

By contrast, develop the ability to level with anybody, regardless of status. The late French philosopher Paul Ricoeur was such a person. I still remember clearly the night I dined with him at a small restaurant in Naples, Italy. Ricoeur looked everyone straight in the eyes, asked questions, and listened for a long time. Then he spoke a few measured words of wisdom. He visibly expressed how much he learned from us. He was in his 90s, an academic monument, still learning every day.

Leadership from below	Introductory Lesson
Learn to lead from below – look beyond the hierarchy.	

Chapter 1

Finding your place of impact

Globalization challenges you. Stimulates you to move around, looking for opportunities. But you still need to be present if you want to have an impact. Leaders choose wisely where to spend their energy. But how and what do you choose?

Knowledge is often unspoken, hidden – the experts say knowledge is tacit.[4] What you know can't always be spelled out. You may not know what you know. You may have too many things on your mind, or too much information in front of you. In short, there are many reasons why knowledge is sticky. A Norwegian aphorism claims that experience is embedded in the walls of the institution. Only by spending time inside the same walls do you access it. Moreover, once you are inside the walls your thinking is constrained. You speak from a fixed position.

By the same token, both the physical and metaphorical walls are the perimeter of what you know, what you can do and say. Certain things are not said. The walls also insulate you from the outside. Public institutions and also larger corporations all have infrastructure. The walls or buildings provide reminders, containing symbolic power. Suffice to think of the Pentagon, the UN, or the Eiffel Tower.

Knowledge is embodied.[5] It usually resides with a person and can only be expressed by that person. Moreover, knowledge is ephemeral, occurring in the blink of insight, only to become irrelevant if it is not picked up there and then.[6] Very often, business knowledge older than six months goes cold and looses much of its relevance. This is certainly true of social networks. Know-how activates when people meet and tasks need to be accomplished; if not, it dies.

Knowledge is produced by combining things in ways that seem a bit odd. From there, you try to convince others that there is some common ground. The Japanese have a name for it − *ba* − a common space for action where participants feel safe and exchange insights that are "actionable."[7] The Japanese management scholar Nonaka used *ba* to describe the innovation that occurred within the Sony Corporation in the early 1990s. Knowledge thrives only if there is a culture fit for it to thrive.

Knowledge needs networks, but networks are just a potential. To put networks to work demands the actions of motivated workers. Innovators must meet each other daily in order to explore and pitch ideas. Successfully persuading someone and finally "freeze" a loose concept into a meaningful picture (what psychologists call a gestalt), is the only way an idea can become a reality. The final phases of negotiation are nearly always offline. Wherever there is dissent, the real life cues of body language, the ability to move around freely, pop into each other's offices to mobilize resources or discuss a matter at hand, the talk by the coffee machine – all trivial things become important. Good decisions are made only when there is trust. Trust can only occur when we relax and let go of our fears. Yet, it is the essence of knowledge.

In IBM, on any given day, only 60 percent of the workforce reports to a traditional office.[8] The rest work from home, at client sites, or are constantly in transit. Studies of economic activities between world cities like New York, London, Tokyo, Frankfurt, or Singapore over the last decade show increased inter-organizational activity and networking. The Spanish sociologist Manuel Castells has described the last decades as an evolution into a "network society." This society has ever more computerized work processes. Employees travel more. Electronic flows enable the exchange of information through and between large cities. Information goes through the Internet, but also through corporate Intranets and other elite information networks. These enable access, communication, and action across great geographical distance.

"If nomads float on the top, they lose influence. Their managers, meanwhile, struggle to hold teams, projects and companies together."

The flipside of a nomadic workforce is a lack of influence over matters that require sustained interaction in one location. If nomads float on the top, they lose that influence. Meanwhile, their managers struggle to hold together teams, projects, and companies.

Globalization from below

There is quite a flow of people, technology, culture, and capital across borders these days. This is what we can observe. However, while the material foundation of social interaction is increasingly mobile, so to speak, the physical encounters between the elite are still important. Are physical places becoming less important?

Flows, especially electronic flows, enable elites and cities to grow in number and importance. The result: a world that will one day function like one, globally networked space in which people are only relevant because of their links.[9] Will that happen? The process will take time

Placemaking – activating your surroundings

While it looks like these flows are what matters, there is actually something else going on. People are engaging in what I will call placemaking[10]. Placemaking is a generic human process. People take in a subset of the possible impressions that are around them and make them their own. Speaking, convincing others, we establish facts and make changes around us.

Placemaking is very physical, as the three people I now discuss will reveal. Chen, 35, is a fashion designer from Singapore. His usage of shopping online is radically different from Julia, 40, a venture capitalist in New York City. Fatima, 16, a schoolgirl in Zambia, could not even dream of shopping at all. To Fatima, the Internet exists to learn about other countries and gain access to books. She wants to grow up to feed her extended family of 15. To Chen, the Internet is all about comparing images of designer fabrics and styles from across the globe to his own designs. To Julia, it is a tool she uses to benchmark possible investments and background information, so she can decide which start-up to invite back for lunch the following week.

The place-making process has three stages: First, like Julia on Wall Street or Fatima in a Zambian school, you need to expose yourself to a site where key things occur. Second, you take part in negotiations ("stirring up") between ideas, meanings, and designs. Fatima cannot merely sit there if she wants to make a difference, learn fast, and develop a drive. Chen knows that too, because his team needs to produce his designs. Julia cannot convince the rest of her team that her analysis is correct and better than her more experienced colleagues. Third, you contribute to "freezing" one chosen approach. You attempt to establish boundaries and consequences. The result is what becomes a concept. However, if Chen gets an idea while taking a shower, that idea is worth nothing unless he successfully pitches it to someone and they act on it.

Knowledge work does have elements of silence and concentration, of freedom to think. But eventually you need to enter into intensive dialogue in order to convince others. Then, you need to pause in order to reflect on the impressions from others. In the middle, there is a constant flow of communication that you need to ignore, but still be able to pick out the bits that require your attention.

Julia lives in New York, works on Wall Street, and interacts with people and computers in a very narrowly defined physical space in lower Manhattan. What matters to her is what matters to those people with whom she shares her profession. She is, of course, watching consumer trends across the globe, but everything is interpreted within her context. Whatever is brought to her attention, and convinces her and the others, counts in her decision-making, everything else does not. In Zambia, for the most part, design is out of scope.

"Knowledge work has elements of silence and concentration, of freedom to think. But eventually you need to enter into intensive dialogue in order to convince others."

Throughout the 1990s, many companies abolished offices in favor of open spaces. They got team offices instead of individual offices, brought in gourmet food, and focused on providing flexible kitchen facilities and common lunch rooms for their employees. They provided more and more basic services. Laundry, shopping, and Kindergarten can now be found on the corporate campus. They even endorsed leisure activities as part of the workday (such as ping-pong, running, and cultural activities).

Why did they do all this, if all is moving electronic? Why do this if innovation could be measured in Web links? Do they miss the social life that everyone else enjoys? Could it be that they compensate for the loss of meaning in their work?

The average American workweek has gone from 40 to 60 hours in just 20 years. In 1998's *The Corrosion of Character*, cultural sociologist Richard Sennett wrote about the personal consequences of losing our lives to businesses that demand more hours than ever before.

Loyalty is lost at the promise of an artificial type of freedom – that of choosing which employers get to drive you to the maximum – until you collapse. Corporations are nowadays taking over functions that previously were handled by the family, the welfare state, the police, or other basic institutions of society. Is that healthy?

Choose your employer wisely. Business culture can make the difference between a sustainable or an unsustainable company. If one were to study old-economy companies like General Electric, one could conclude that keeping core values and changing specific goals and strategies is part of the same game.[11] Look at the best employer rankings and figure out what counts the most for you.

Leading knowledge work

Knowledge work consists partly of non-social practices essentially aimed at isolating oneself (e.g., thinking, concentrating, etc.) and partly of social practices (e.g., thinking, pushing, and pitching). The knowledge work process, if you wish, comprises several steps.

First, you try to make sense of things around you – your thoughts and ideas – and the tasks you are given. This step happens not only during billable hours in your office or with a customer, but also it occurs at home, when traveling, in cafés -- in short, also on your free time. Technology is seldom the only driving force in this process; it's merely one element for you to consider.[12]

Second, you mobilize your own energy, acting upon your insight, trying to convince others, and setting out to create and establish facts. In fact, what we regard as true is based on knowledge we trust -- and nothing else.

Third, there is the step where you design the final format of the paper, the speech, or the product you are making. In this final step, you write out the "manuscript" for someone else to act upon, your instructions for use. If you are a designer, you try to let the instructions be "invisible" and self-evident from seeing the product itself. If you have taken enough care to think of the customer, he or she will use it the intended way, otherwise not.

In a famous case of folly, development workers brought electronic lamp devices to an African country only to realize that there were no replacement parts on the continent. The product was clearly designed for a society with larger product supply. All products are designed for a purpose.

If you are reading this book, you are likely to have a house or an apartment you call your own, whether you actually own it or not. Humans tend to produce meaningful attachment to people, places, and objects in order to feel safe and to feel they are in place, at home, and at ease. Placemaking activates those otherwise ephemeral knowledge bits. Through our pitching initiatives and efforts, talking about it, we convince people and stabilize things around us. Psychology is clear on the matter – control is a human need. Leaders understand psychology, while managers do not.

Leadership from below	Lesson #1
Be present where knowledge is found, products are made, and markets are shaped. Re-shape those surroundings and make the most out of every situation. Look around you and do what successful peers do.	

Chapter 2

Tapping into power from below

More than formal authority, leaders need thinking, persuading, and even pitching skills. Anybody can acquire and refine these skills. But patience is required. Ideally you start early, and practice daily.

*I*f only three skills are needed to succeed, what exactly are they? Thinking is when you calmly prepare, and also when you smartly adjust. Persuading is when you explore a product idea with others to figure out whether you have something that merits development. Pitching is when you sell and present a packaged product. None of these skills are merely a matter of cognitive ability, or IQ. All of them can be learned. Nobody can succeed in their career by only mastering one or two of them.

Thinking – and emotional support

Management professor Thomas H. Davenport's book *Thinking for a Living: How to Get Better Performance and Results from Knowledge Workers* (2005) has one good point: Thinking plays an important role in knowledge work. But his notion of thinking is fairly limited. Thinking is not an abstract activity of the mind. Rather, it entails actively interacting – making the mind and body interact – in a professional environment, trying to understand markets, relationships, technologies, and people. That is where leadership and thinking merge. Neither is efficient in isolation.

"Chance encounters are a crucial part of innovation"

Pondering, reflecting, and selecting – all of these cognitive processes are involved in thinking. The activities those processes lead to, however, include gathering information from reading, conversation, or observation. Thinking is not only about having a clear mind. Louis Pasteur wrote, "In the fields of observation, chance favors only the prepared mind."[13] Some analytical skills we are born with, others develop if stimulated well in childhood and as we attend schools and colleges, or confront life circumstances. Cognitive psychology says that intelligence is a good measure of how quickly you process information. Effective knowledge workers have set preferences for what information they deem relevant, and they devise means to deal with enormous amount of input, selecting what matters from what does not. Thinking is the process by which we calibrate that selection.

The professional and personal habits of a leader merge. What matters, according to French sociologist Pierre Bourdieu, is to form an educated habitus – the unconscious preferences that guide our search. Habitus is the collection of all of our habits developed over time. Only occasionally are they spelled out as analytic principles. Thinking is almost automatic at times. At other times, thinking hurts, especially if you are stretching your mind trying out counterintuitive ideas that challenge the status quo. The results might be uncomfortable.

Leaders, however global in outlook, are bounded in particular places. They are human beings who need attention, care, inspiration, and motivation from a small number of people around them. In order for that to happen, physical infrastructure is often needed. You will find many leaders in large cities like New York, London, Paris, or Tokyo, and in the financial district of those cities, as well as in the skyscrapers of those districts, and finally in the proximity of bars, theatres, hotels, Wi-Fi and broadband connections. More importantly, leaders need to be in the proximity of managers who engage with them on a daily basis -- not only by sending emails, but also by interacting; not only in meetings, but also on the way to meetings, right after the meetings, on the way to lunch, even in the restroom. Like most people, leaders need emotional support. They need to feel motivated, needed, and unique. Good assistants do that. Good peers, too.

Leaders do not want to be controlled. You deliver a great deal, but only if left alone until you are ready to communicate. Inventing new concepts is challenging not only for the mind, but also for our emotional state. It feels threatening to launch your own ideas. We have fear that they will not be accepted, in which case it sometimes feels like we are ourselves being rejected. Leaders are, this way, beginning to experience the symptoms previously felt mostly by poets and writers.

You may work very well with others but still face problems when confronted with your own projects. In this day and age, with more action, faster processes, and demands from all sides, many find the biggest challenge is how to concentrate. Providing yourself with the right environment to think – following what we have said above – is not always enough. In the end, you need to produce something. How do you ensure you are thinking creatively? How do you concentrate?

Most people have favorite spots where they are creative, often where they are undisturbed for a long period of time. This way, the flow process is not interrupted.

Your creativity and energy can occur at favorite times of day – for some it is the morning, for others it is the evening. For most people, morning is the time of peak energy. Make sure the entire morning is not spent in administrative meetings. If you are meeting people, it should be for strategic meetings, high-stakes customer meetings, or brainstorming sessions.

"Let me tell you the secret that has led me to my goal: my strength lies solely in my tenacity" – Louis Pasteur

Thinking skills must be honed. You need to develop good habits that constantly challenge your own thinking and that may be confronted by others. If your current environment does not give you such stimuli, you must change something. Otherwise you will not keep the edge.

Persuading – in the presence of others

Nothing happens if you sit alone, ponder, and never get out -- or, if you never share, test, or grind your ideas against reality. Products are honed in discussion with others. When you have to defend your point of view and hold your own, you improve. Pushing ideas forward in a discussion with others, against resistance, being challenged, are all part of testing the validity of a thought.

People who try to obtain a patent have to fight for it. They have to prove it is a unique, original invention. If you are an entrepreneur seeking capital for your start-up company, you have to visit many venture capitalists before the first commits her capital.

The possibility of face-to-face interaction is crucial to knowledge creation and successful knowledge work. Not for nothing, eyewitness accounts traditionally bear a great deal of weight in court. Face-to-face work is about transforming tacit knowledge – things you did not know that you knew. The persuasion process consists of hard-sell convincing: first, you pitch the idea to someone, then stir up conceptual energy in order to peak his attention. Then, to ensure his attention is sustained, put the idea into action, sculpting and refining it, while crucially retaining the initial shape. If you have invited six dinner guests to your table, you cannot serve ready-made stuff with success. Rather, you carefully select ingredients. You follow a recipe, improvise, and follow through based on previous successful dishes.

Brainstorming only works when people are openly letting ideas flow. A real brainstorming session is a rare occurrence that requires suspending judgment; thinking out of the box; saying everything that comes to mind; recording all ideas; building on ideas; and, finally, analyzing the results. When people are pushing each other, it works -- otherwise, you are better off alone or contributing ideas into a pool and letting one person deal with it.

Failure of brainstorming is common. Involving everyone at all times is not easy. Free riders waste your time. Waiting time can block energy rather than release it. And at the end of an unsuccessful brainstorming session, the focus on output leads to a phenomenon called anchoring – attaching too much meaning to the last idea mentioned. Time pressure, a common occurrence, can be totally destructive. Free thought takes any amount of time and then it is done. Brainstorms usually are on a schedule – because people are.

Leading ideas emerge only when successfully activate a hyperspace – an area of total attention – around our flow of information. People move around, and, because of books and the Internet, so does information. But knowledge does not move easily. Knowledge is only relevant if it convinces others. Physical co-presence is therefore important. How else can you create the type of hyperspace intensity needed for knowledge transfer? Leaders exploit this fact. They carefully select where and with whom to spend their time.

Pitching – the art of efficient delivery

In 2006, when Boston's famous baseball team, the Red Socks, posted a record $51.1 million bid for the Japanese pitcher Daisuke Matsuzaka, they knew what they were doing. He throws harder, with better control, than others, and he uses his body to achieve velocity, not his arm. More importantly, the Red Socks now have an incredible hand capable of keeping his hitters frustrated and guessing, masterfully switching between his near 100 mph fastball, his off-speed pitch, and his breaking ball, with pin-point control -- nearly always pitching right into the strike zone. Clearly, there is a *Zen* to pitching. Moreover, Matsuzaka is a brand that grows every day.

To lead, thinking is not enough. Emotional support from mentors, family, teachers, managers, or investors, or team discussions are not enough. Persuading each other is not enough. Precise delivery – pitching – the presenting, selling, and shortening of messages, is crucial. Pitching efforts require both online and offline spacemaking. You may need to work for hours to shorten and refine your slide presentation, nailing the action words, removing the superfluous. This is why you need to practice tomorrow's presentation in the mirror. Tape it and play it back to prevent stuttering. You prepare your pitch by warming up the audience days beforehand; Sending them short emails, popping by their office, and telling the joke of the day. Whatever you do, make sure they remember you are there, but don't bother people. Influential people are never for a minute forgotten. Nor do they come off as pushy. Everyone understands how important he is.[14]

Knowledge is not a thing you can store easily. There are books that may give you really useful information – but only if you read it the right way and at the right time. There are databases that have lots of information and can assist in acquiring information. In practice, however, knowledge is ephemeral. It is there, and then it disappears. In fact, knowledge is a relationship. You can think of friendship. You know if you have it. You maintain it and you keep it and you are fine. If it gets lost, you will know quickly, and it can seldom be restored.

Innovation is rooted in place-bound activity. Even most so-called virtual encounters take place with people's paramount reality being the awareness of their own location. People are unable to fully detach themselves from their physical environment for very long. Even a hacker needs to eat. Hackers have been known to make love offline. Research shows that virtual teams need to build a relationship by face-to-face encounters before they can collaborate effectively. Often, they need to reinforce relationships before, during, and after such processes are over.

Headquartered in London, HSBC is one of the largest banking and financial services organizations in the world. HSBC Group, an international network of more than 9,800 offices in 77 countries and territories across the world, prides itself on being the world's local bank. Market presence can never be completely mediated, even though some products sell online. You have to be as close as possible to important customers to answer to their demands and pick up new consumer trends. Full market presence is still not completely virtually enabled.

Urban work settings seen in cities like San Francisco, or even the intimate tech tinseltown of Trondheim, Norway, where Google, FAST, and Yahoo! have set up their software development labs, provide extrinsic motivation by ways of coffeehouses, pubs, and meeting places within walking distance. In fact, the sustained effort made possible through presence, generally, enables the knowledge worker always to try again, insist, and return to his fellow knowledge workers, competitors, or investors and to enjoy serendipitous encounters. The urban complexity of New York City, Tokyo, Rio di Janeiro, London, Jakarta, or Beijing facilitates foreign, multicultural, and diverse encounters. Results are often innovative.

High-tech innovation also occurs in advanced but isolated places like high-tech office parks or a Fortune 500 corporation's headquarters. Those companies try to create a utopia within its own borders. Cisco is a good example. Caught in its own Cisco village in the meadows outside San Jose, California, the urban complexity does not exist. Workers are condemned to themselves, alike in socio-economic status, and with matching interests, albeit in sunny California. However, while some diversity is also found within a company campus, the effervescence of "place" will come into play immediately upon leaving it. In fact, it may be intensified. The shopping and bar strip outside the gates of most American military bases outside the United States is evidence of that. The absence of free markets inside the base leads to an extreme market immediately outside. The Mexico-U.S. border town of Tijuana is another example – everything Californians think is Mexican is maximized.

Due to the intensity of knowledge exchanges, cultural institutions that bring with them a flow of impressions, and diversity of people, cities like San Francisco become havens of exotic knowledge. Swedish urban anthropologist Ulf Hannerz claims that because of all the African immigrants and the educational institutions in Europe and the United States, Africa is paradoxically more available and easier to understand abroad than from Zambia (although the experience is certainly not the same).

Can placemaking only happen in urban settings? Of course not, but the probability is greater because the urban center contains many impressions in a limited physical space. A weekend hike in the mountains with colleagues or friends can also be educational, if the place or the colleagues are interesting.

Leadership from below	Lesson #2
Leaders without formal authority need thought, persuasiveness, and a good pitch. With these you can master any situation	

Chapter 3

Becoming a speed-reader

The average reader of English spends about one month reading a book. In fact, many never finish at all. The average reader's speed is approximately 200 words per minute and he or she will comprehend enough to remember the gist of the argument and a lot of quite unhelpful detail. Speed reading, used sparingly, can change that altogether.

Anyone can learn speed-reading. It is a trained art. Having put myself through a rigorous training program for several months, I have found that I can average more than 1,000 words per minute if desired. On average, I try to read about 100 books per year. If I have to cover more ground -- for instance, working on an intense project -- I can read up to ten books per day.

Speed-readers are successful. Most great leaders of the twentieth century have been speed-readers. John F. Kennedy could read several thousand words per minute. I am not saying you should aim to match that, but anyone who takes speed-reading seriously will improve drastically in a matter of months. The first principle of speed-reading is: practice, practice, practice. You will get nowhere simply knowing the principles. And the principles are not always the same as the ones you learned in first grade. The texts have changed as well. The online environment poses additional challenges.

Speed is the single most important skill in terms of reading, but it is not the only one. Reading fast is no substitute for making sure you understand the meaning. The psychology of memory tells you that the brain will process new elements by attaching them to known or similar memories. Comprehension is a process that starts with the sense impressions but continues in the immediate hours after exposure to books and ideas. Therefore, beyond speed, what matters is to have strategies to structure your thoughts after you have gotten this exposure.

But it does not always help to slow down -- and, the way knowledge work is going, you may not have the choice. There is just too much information to digest, and little time. You can choose to ignore it, but only at your own peril. On the other hand, prioritizing becomes a more and more valued skill. The British philosopher John Stuart Mill is said to be the last person to have known and read everything available to read and know. Whether or not that was true, he died in 1873 -- long before the Internet. Now, all you can hope for is to read the most relevant information in a small field of expertise -- and even that is becoming hard to do:

Just ask top university professors or scientists in corporate laboratories.

There are several reading modes, and you should use them depending on what you want to accomplish. The six important modes are: glancing, skimming, searching, experiencing, reflecting, and memorizing. When glancing, you may finish entire books in literally a glance at the title; when memorizing, you may spend up to five minutes per word.

Glancing – letting impressions flow

Glancing is when you are just curious about a book but do not yet know whether it is worth buying, loaning, or stealing for a moment. Amazon.com's "Search Inside!" feature caters to this activity by letting you browse some immediate features of a book – its cover, index, introduction, and conclusion.

The efficient knowledge worker will browse through books, sorting through the relevant categories for him or her at that moment – catchy title, appealing cover, innovative idea, etc. -- but also storing some of this awareness for future reference. While the idea here is not necessarily to maximize the word comprehension per minute, speed is a factor. The important thing is to relax, even though you are trying to make a decision that will affect your wallet, your time, and your career.

The problem with this activity is that the range of choices is so immense, it's often overwhelming. Especially to a knowledge worker who likes to feel that she or he has an overview of all relevant information at a given time. Some pointers:

- Immerse yourself fully for a good amount of time – in uninterrupted flow

- Relax. Take breaks. Assess what you have found for a moment.

- Decide what to do. Write down the ideas you culled. Purchase, loan, or discard.

Skimming – a musical performance

Skimming is when you are interested in the overall idea of a book or a text, or are just scanning through large amounts of information looking for particular concepts, key words, or names. The clue here is to keep a steady rhythm, but vary the speed -- slowing down when you find something potentially interesting, speeding up or skipping full chunks of text when those indications are there. This process is much like performing a musical piece in which you set your own tempo, dynamics, and mood (*al piacere*), gradually slowing down (*ritardando*), or accelerating (*accelerando*), or varying dynamics from very softly (*pianissimo*) to loudly (*fortissimo*).[15] You may think of reading as a type of performance; in fact, you may read aloud whenever you feel like it, or whisper if it aids your comprehension or adds to the experience.

Searching – finding the match

Searching is when you are looking for something in particular based on some preset requirements. Just keep what you are looking for present in your mind with only a small opening for other relevant things you may discover underway, and start with flipping through libraries or bookshelves, or plotting in strategically chosen words and synonyms in search engines.

Searching mode is prevalent in the online environment, and we discuss the technological features of search engines in another chapter. Searching skills vary greatly even among advanced knowledge workers. Generally, people are better at finding things within their own domain of expertise and may be terrible at searching outside it. Things to remember:

- Select a search engine tailored to your type of search. While Google, Yahoo!, or MSN are popular, there are thousands of other free engines on the Web, depending on your purpose.

- Use the advanced features of the search engine, experimenting with different settings and key words. Store your searches so you don't repeat the same search every time. If the engine allows it, set automatic searches and have them delivered to a dedicated email or Web page. Having found Web pages you need, choose your social book marking software (e.g., del.cio.us or Digg)[16] to store and share links.

- Make sure you have reduced the number of hits drastically before you start considering each result. When you find data, spend enough time so that you fully comprehend the source, content, authenticity and value.

- Humans are better than machines: ask someone who is insightful

Experiencing

Avid readers often resist speed-reading because it comes across as a technique. On the contrary, speed-reading is also about reading slowly. When you want to experience a text, you must slow down to a comfortable speed, which will vary depending on your skills, your mood, the time of day, and the type of text you have before you. Treating the text as a full experience is important -- for instance, when it's purely for enjoyment and personal satisfaction, when you are trying to enjoy or even assess its aesthetic or artistic merits, or when you are finding yourself immersed in a text that is particularly innovative and thought-provoking. When getting into this mode, the following is important:

- Take away all other things that may interrupt you – ignore phone calls, kids, spouses, TV, emails, and all the rest: Enter flow.
- Complement the experience with other similar activities before and after, arousing the same emotions or building on them.
- Dwell on each word for a while (especially if reading a poem); look for the imagery it evokes; take in the thoughts and feelings aroused by the text.
- Write down your impressions on the white part of the page, in the back of the book, on a Post-it note, in the PDA, or in your own notebook or diary. Ideally, you then will go back to them, structure them into larger texts, and store them electronically on your blog, so that you can share your thoughts.

Reflecting

Some texts present you with clear choices. You may create a slide presentation or write a text arguing for this or the other strategy or purchase. In this case, you may have to reflect in the absence of the text. That is, you read through it in the speed that you see fit, and then you take a break, and revisit it later. In this instance, your goal is to find the ideal time to put it away and to know how much time you need to process the choice subconsciously. The time required will be roughly corresponding to the enormity of the choice –you need more time if it's more complex – but it also is a matter of personal preference and habit. Some things to remember are:

- Remember your own successful habits. What did you do the last time you know you made a good decision or reflected on an issue? Where were you? To whom did you talk?

- Incorporate the new with your previous knowledge. How does it tie in?

Memorizing

These days, memorization is very rarely required. If it is, there are many mnemonic techniques to assist you beyond simply repeating words out loud until they are stuck in your head. For example:

- Linking words, names, and concepts you don't know to something you do know – and that bears some resemblance, is funny together, reminds you of the other, or begins with the same letter.

- Dividing the task into components that are easier to handle. Look for recurring patterns in the text you need to memorize. Visualize where they belong in the text. Memorize the rest.

Reading speed – the technical skills

Technical skills are important (e.g., strategic eye movements, handling the book, and page turning if offline -- and juggling many windows and hyperlinked threads when online). This is the part you need to practice. Depending on your starting point, here is some advice:

- Commit to 20-minute trainings sessions every day for a month or two with monitored reading exercises. Time these exercises, and chart your progress.

- You may want to purchase a book on speed-reading, but you can also use your own material and follow these steps, designing your own program.

Week 1 – Eye movement and speed

Average readers read every word just as they appear in the sentence, never skipping any words and with about the same speed all the time.

Try to read a text without reading every word. Instead, focus on the action verbs -- the substantives as well as the negations. You also need to know what to look for, dividing the text into meaningful components.

Try to grasp a whole paragraph in one go. Practice moving your eye rapidly across the whole paragraph, not just line for line. In the beginning, you will try to read two lines at a time; later in the week, you must try to read in zigzag, from the top right toward the middle of the paragraph on the left, then flip backward. If you think about it, word order is not so important to the brain. In German sentences, for instance, words are ordered very differently from English sentences, and Germans seem to still get the meaning (among other things, Germans have the advantage of a more precise grammar). You just need to get used to it.

What will happen after a while is that your area of active vision will expand. Our eyes have a great capacity to take in impressions, but we seldom use them to their potential.

Week 2 – Finger movements

Practice using your index finger to point at the text. Your teacher told you not to do this, and he was right, since pointing to each word slows down reading -- that is, when you read line for line with the help of your finger. However, when reading entire paragraphs and, later, full book pages, the finger is a necessary tool. As you will discover, rapid finger technique is also is a key to changing pages fast.

Week 3 – Expanding online comprehension

If you can increase the number of online window menus open and still can track what is going on, you will increase your information processing speed, in effect, by several hundred words a minute, maybe even thousands of words.

The trick is this: Start with assessing your regular habits (say, having an email window open and a few windows while you search, in addition to a text editor and maybe a messenger client). Increase the number of windows by 20 percent, either by adding another feature or by adding more search windows, the latter of which is probably easier. Then time yourself executing a search for a concept, say "knowledge management" or "terrorism." Beforehand, you have decided some search parameters, so you have a target. Now, try following up on at least three threads at the same time; click on hyperlinks on each thread until there are so many windows open that you loose track. Write down your experiences and what your limit was, and also assess your findings. Is the quality of your search still good? Put it away, and do the same exercise the next day, with a different search term. On the third day, use the original search term and compare your results.

Incidentally, playing computer games has about the same effect on expanding visual multi-processing skills as any of these exercises. If you prefer that, please do so. In fact, this is why your children may never have to take a speed-reading course. They may, however, run into the problem of concentration – which is also an essential part of knowledge work.

Week 4 – Applying your skills

In the last week of the program, you must apply your skills to your real-life challenges. Just take a work assignment, a new project idea, your leisure reading, whatever it is, and spend the week writing down your experiences with treating them in this new way, noting your preferred and maximum processing speeds and testing your own comprehension.

If you execute this program, we promise that the results will be satisfying. Speed-reading will improve your leadership skills, as you will develop an increased capacity to multi-task and to process information better, more quickly, and more precisely. You maximum reading speed will at least double, and your enjoyment of reading -- both offline and online -- will increase. It is definitely worth a try.

For a more in-depth focus on speed-reading, consult the bibliography and endnotes.[17]

Leadership from below	Lesson # 3
Keep learning key skills, such as speed reading, and practice daily the six important modes: glancing, skimming, searching, experiencing, reflecting, and memorizing. Never again will you be overwhelmed by document piles or strategy papers.	

*C*hapter 4

Getting access

Every leader dreams of being wanted everywhere. How to use the journalistic, the therapeutic, and the investigative mindsets? Develop a natural way to communicate with everyone you meet. Leadership from below gives you instant access to the elite.

*T*oday, the average person knows hundreds of people. Many of us know thousands in passing, and we meet tens of thousands throughout our lives. What counts is not the number itself but, rather, meeting the right person at the right time – both in business and pleasure. Increasingly, work is about whom you meet and what you get out of the meet. This brings us to those you may want to meet: the powerful, the elite, the unique -- in short, those who generally are hard to find.

Traditionally, the elite operate powerful networks by heritage, merit, or circumstances. However, increasingly, elite impact is quite invisible. The most influential might not appear that way and vice versa. Leaders know how to find, access, and interview elites as a matter of course.

Access implies inside knowledge. Gaining access is a precarious, ongoing, and renegotiable process. It never ends. Your network will not stay fresh forever. Your status may change as time passes. People move along. The perception that you are able to deliver useful perspectives may change. Access is time-consuming. You must cope with organizational gatekeepers who constrain you in various ways.

"You gain access if you have something to say and something desirable to offer"

The leadership from below perspective is perfect for meeting up with the elite, because it is non-threatening. You see yourself as a leader but not as better than anyone else. You see yourself as having a right to question most things, but you are not a troublemaker. You see yourself as a people person, but you are not a cynical networker who preys on contacts alone. Leaders never use people. Rather, they influence, shape, and make people feel important – especially if they are.

You gain access if and when you have something to say. You need a message. And you need to one of these desirable things to offer: money, prestige, power, insight, knowledge, advice, attractiveness, politeness, listening skills – or just a good conversation. Then, you need to underbid others. As a generic strategy, focus on getting access to people whom you do not yet know. Target the gatekeepers to the insights you are seeking.

According to sociologist Manuel Castells, the increasing value of networks and knowledge workers is bringing about new network elite. The new elite consist of "switchers" (i.e., people who have the possibility to open or shut off your access to networks of people or information). For example, you may control undergraduate admission at Stanford University – which can make or break careers. Or you may be an executive of Telenor, the former state telecommunications firm that controls almost all Internet access to the Kingdom of Norway.

The elite have a huge amount of what Stanford sociologist Mark Granovetter, in a seminal 1973 article, labeled "weak ties." These are potential social relationships that extend your networks exponentially in an important direction. Weak ties are not friends but, rather, contacts that may suddenly become important to you if you know how to use them.

In a timeless *New Yorker* article penned in 1999, Malcolm Gladwell, author of *Blink* and *The Tipping Point*, wrote about a Chicago woman he calls Lois Weinberg, who introduces everyone she meets to somebody else. Her parties are legendary for this reason. After all, who does not want this kind of attention? She is a switcher, standing "at the intersection of different worlds, connecting people, creating opportunities, and spreading ideas," wrote Gladwell. All of us know at least one Lois Weinberg. Be one yourself.

Leadership from below spans domains, sectors, age cohorts, and countries. The 55+ age set are quickly finding that their Kiwanis, Rotary, or Elks memberships, industry associations, Masons, and old-boy private networks, no longer guarantee access to knowledge and opportunities. More flexible networks, such as business school alumni networks, go some of the way. Online networks like LinkedIn, Plaxo or Facebook can help structuring who you know and staying in touch with them more easily. But to stay competitive, you have to work on whom you know all the time. Even if you do, you cannot talk to everybody you want to.

While weak ties are valuable in themselves, what counts, in the end, is to convincingly convey the *assumption* that you have inside connections. Failing that, you must rely on your persistence, social skills, and improvisation. Access always involves face-to-face negotiation and demands time, effort and risk. Access is often granted to people who are perceived to have the right mindset -- and blocked to others who might indeed be smarter or more experienced.

We will now briefly explore three successful mindsets exhibited by leaders: the journalistic, the therapeutic, and the investigative.[18]

The Journalistic Mode

The International Federation of Journalists, the world's largest, has 500,000 members in more than 100 countries. There are of course far more journalists in the world. In some ways, we should all be journalists, at least part of the day.

The journalistic approach is intuitive. Journalists are quick, active, and persistent. The journalist is not afraid to ask. He or she will insist on getting an interview. Journalists accustomed to working through acquaintances, contacts, friends, and secretaries.

It is always important to let people know whom and what you represent. For most people, affiliation is the first level of screening. You must always remember which of your affiliations is more efficient and suits the occasion. Big is not always beautiful. Hans-Wilhelm Steinfeld, a leading Norwegian journalist we interviewed, confirms that power dynamics and improvisation determine access to power:

> *I always had the privilege of representing the Norwegian Broadcasting Corporation. It is small, but respected. In the middle of May of 1980, there was a meeting between the American and Soviet foreign ministers in Vienna. Kevin O'Ryan from BBC and I went against the current, ignored the announced American press conference, and placed ourselves outside of Hofburg castle to try for Andrej Gromyko, who eventually emerged. I approached Gromyko by pointing to my colleague, asking whether BBC and Norwegian TV could get a question. Gromyko looked distastefully at my BBC colleague and said in English, "Oh, yes -- BBC, the organization which thinks it knows everything in the world." I quickly pointed to myself and asked whether or not the little, and innocent, TV station NRK from Oslo then could ask the questions instead. I got a six-minute interview."*

Now, what can we learn from this story? Many who refuse an interview are in reality afraid of not having enough interesting things to say to you. Contrary to what it might seem like, if you are famous or have a privileged position, a controversial reputation would interfere with access. When access is granted, what people say will be influenced by who you are. For this reason, famous people get different interviews than the not-so-famous.

Secondly, Steinfeld cleverly uses the authority of the BBC representative, then twists it to his advantage, distancing himself from him when he finds out this does not work. Gromyko feels that big broadcasting companies have too much influence and was reluctant to always give in to their demands. He knows he cannot always control the situation. Steinfeld turns this around, using Gromyko's own logic of allying himself with the little guy. He created an instant connection, one in which Gromyko again feels dominant.

Harvard psychologist Howard Gardner has found social intelligence to be a separate skill, comprising intrapersonal and interpersonal skills. Moreover, in leadership, emotional intelligence is required – the ability to recognize the feelings of others as well as your own. The concept of emotional intelligence was explored in 1995 by popular psychologist Daniel Goleman. Most of all, what matters is to give exclusive attention. Nothing else is as flattering as that. Nothing will encourage a person open up to you as much as careful, but active, listening. According to the psychoanalyst Faimberg, in this way, listening becomes a form of activity.

The Gromyko example tells us that interviews are power situations; there are psychological factors at play, which we now will explore.

The Therapeutic Mode

While all of us think we know what a therapist does, you don't really know unless you have been treated by one. For better or for worse, a large percentage of us will see one in our lifetime. More importantly, therapists perform a function that is in demand – that of *real* listening.

Establishing rapport is about gaining trust. Leaders grasp the situation at hand without being noticed. Leaders use their intuition to uncover layers of knowledge, much like the psychotherapist. Leaders are observant. When you meet someone, try to find out things that others do not know. Make sure you are not the one doing all the talking. The important thing is to listen – not just to what the other person says, but also to the way the other person listens to you. To what does he or she respond? If you say this, what do they respond? How is that different from others? What does that tell you about that person? What could be his or her basic drivers? Of what are they afraid? What makes them proud?

Once you have the answer to some of those questions in your mind, you probe them: "You seem to be interested in X, which is fascinating. Tell me more."

Many interviews become easier after you get going: If you let someone talk about herself, she relaxes. Everyone loves to have an audience for his own ideas and someone to listen to his experiences. If you manage to find a topic that is dear to your subject, steer the interview in that direction for a while. Interview guru Grant McCracken (1988) says a good interview launches "Grand Tour" questions – big, open questions with narrative answers. The answers are rich in information and context, often richer than people realize. Successfully posing open questions like that allow you to sit back and ride on one or a small set of questions alone. The only problem is that you may need to dig for a while to find what you are looking for. The answers won't spring from your prepared list of questions; grand tour questions take time and patience.

I have often found myself totally fascinated and immersed in the world of the person to whom I am talking, while trying to establish a connection. One example is my interview of "John," one of the top industrialists in Leksvika, an industrial township in Norway. I brought a colleague along to show strength. We were impressed with what John and his father had built up through the years, and we made no secret about it. We expressed our fascination with what he called the "industrial adventure" – a term we adopted and repeated several times, almost like a mantra. As a result, John took the time to give us anecdotes and detailed insights far beyond the timeframe we had arranged. We learned that their business was never the same: "We change all the time," says John. "Markets change fast. On one of our products, 'Elsafe,' we lost all of the €4 million invested. Then, from 1989 onward, it became a success. We could sell 90,000 safes a year." We also learned that even the guy at the local bank had entrepreneurial instincts. When things became tough ("And they always do!"), the banker did not panic but, rather, worked with the entrepreneurs through the crisis. Finally, John says, "Business is about creating self-confidence and making sure that spreads to others. My father was the charismatic center in any crowd." His meetings were canceled that day. John felt flattered and gave us the interview in appreciation. The interview became the backbone of our reflection from that point forward. John embodied the social entrepreneurial spirit we had been looking for. We had listened – almost – like therapists.

On another occasion, I drove for two and a half hours each way to interview Inger, the county governor, a senior politician who was a member of the Norwegian legislature Storting between 1977 and 1993, and with unique insight about the regional innovation dynamics we were investigating at the time. Despite her busy schedule, we spent three hours together, during which she shared her experiences building relationships across sectors, breeding deer, and hosting political parties. Why did she give me so much time? She simply explained, "If you came such a long way, you must think this is important. Then I do, too."

So, leaders should see the interview as an opportunity for an honest exchange of views that can make people feel important, comfortable, and at ease. The expectation that they will be heard is usually the rationale for giving access in the first place. Building relationships is what power is all about.

The Investigative Mode

The investigator is on television every day. People are fascinated. But who has the time to develop such skills, anyway? Who has the energy to use them in your professional life?

Leaders should learn from historians who can give an accurate account of the turn of events. Know how to tell a story with the necessary details to make it interesting. Detectives have the skeptical attitude – their gut is to believe nothing until it makes sense to them. For example, you may encounter the political type. Then, you will receive filtered, quick sound bites, clichéd, prepared responses prepared for TV, not for people. If you do not know how to process that, you are left with nothing new.

The investigative mode consists of a detailed inquiry. Pressure makes the truth come out. The main strategies of the cognitive interview – a term usually reserved for police interrogations, military briefs, lawyers' interviews with clients, or testimonials – could usefully be applied by leaders, too.

Leaders in the investigative mode try to uncover as many facts as possible, but without necessarily revealing the aim of the investigation. You always start with non-threatening questions here as well: You start by asking things you do not necessarily care to know. Then, gradually, you narrow your focus on the topic, asking questions about the chronology, context, and precise nature of the event. You need to get the other's mind working, inspire him or her to impress you with detailed knowledge. Emphasize the value of explaining everything: "Nothing is unimportant."

When investigating, you must arrive prepared with facts and angles that will demonstrate insider knowledge. Impress your interviewee. Contribute to the story. Make the interviewee look good. Even so, make him or her remember more, using props. In film, television, and theatre, a prop (short for "property") is any object that gives the scenery, actors, or performance space specific period, place, or character. Similarly, bringing a prop to a public-speaking performance and to interviews can kick start memory (e.g., the document you want to discuss, a business card, or a name

on a piece of paper). You can also deliberately present false facts to
give your interviewee the opportunity to correct you: "I have heard
X. Does that mean Y?"

As soon as you discover that your subject is deliberately lying,
you need to get tough. More often, you are simply presented a
partial account. In either case, leaders may then need to show some
cards. Point out where opinions differ and ask clarification. If you
do not get what you want, you may want to suggest that there are
others who will be more helpful. People respond to that kind of
mild threat, because, having spoken to you for more than ten
minutes, they already seek your approval.

For example, once in the United States, my wife observed a
difficult political situation between the director of a bipartisan high
level fellowship program and the human resources director of
another agency. The director, not knowing that the HR director
and she had already met, claimed a conversation that I know she
did not have. Instead of confronting her with the truth, she simply
let it go. But in the process, it became obvious what had transpired,
and my wife won the argument.

Mix and match to maximize access

With practice, the three mindsets may overlap quite naturally. The
ideal would be to keep switching between them, adapting as you go
along. The *journalistic mindset* captures the ephemeral nature of
things on the go – its strength lies in being there, bearing witness,
and then concluding without further ado. The *investigative mindset*
digs deeper, is suspicious and penetrates commonplace, faulty, or
concealing behavior – its strength is to provide context. The
therapeutic mindset repairs aggressiveness by treating the interview as
an honest human exchange – its strength is the potential for deep,
lasting, and real connections with people.

Using allies both to get in and to ensure continued access is wise. Try to find some commonalties between you and the person you are trying to reach. Provide quick and easy follow-ups that go right to the point. Any salesman will tell you that if the potential sale is large enough, he will be persistent and will not give up. Almost anybody will give in if you take the time. Once, after 15 phone calls, three faxes, and three emails by two team members, I finally got through to a famous European merchant. The secretary admitted that she had grown tired of us and, therefore, asked her boss to grant us an interview.

Usually, when gatekeepers try to keep you out, they do not state their real reasons. What really is going on in their heads, apart from generally not wanting to be disturbed, could be one of these: (1)"I don't know who you are"; (2) "I don't have anything to say"; or (3) "I don't see what's in it for me."

The answer to "I don't know who you are," which will seldom be uttered outright, is subtly to clarify who you are and why you should matter to the person you want to interview. Demonstrate that you are familiar with someone or something your potential interviewee cares about.

The answer to "I don't have anything to say" is to address the interviewee's performance expectations. Instead, clarify that even small details contribute to the larger picture. The elite may also fear having nothing to say (e.g., experts to whom you might want to ask questions outside their area of expertise). In this scenario, ensure that you are not perceived as threatening. Say you think it is important to find out why he or she is silent on this matter.

The answer to "I don't see what's in it for me" is to change your approach. Distribute different types rewards – allude to the effect on their power, influence, visibility, potential fame -- or play on their fears (e.g., what if they do not say something and others do?). You have to increase the stakes. Make it seem important.

If you work for a highly reputable institution, you've experienced the opposite problem: Everybody wants to come if you call. Too many people call, and you are faced with having to reject or limit the contact. Having been on both sides gives important insight, but it does not change the fact that, once you do not work there anymore, you cannot always use the institution's power without twisting the fact. And, even when inside, there are things outside your domain, in which you are a novice – such as when complaining about the phone bill, going on the first date after a divorce, receiving a diagnosis from your auto mechanic, or buying your first house.

Getting from access to knowledge

Merely getting access is never enough. Mastery of trends, developments, and strategies is what gives competitive advantage. Every encounter with a potential contact, a customer, or even your boss should be conceived of as an interview. Why? In the interview, you are never the main person; the interviewee is. Thinking this way helps you transfer attention away from yourself to the person who matters the most to your interviewee: her own self.

The interview itself can be seen as a process with three elements: (1) the opening; (2) the grand tour; and (3) the follow-up. The opening calls for the therapeutic mindset. Sensitivity and social intelligence are necessary to grasp the situation. You must be able to create the right social setting for the interview. Posing the right grand tour question calls for all three mindsets – journalistic, therapeutic, and investigative. The follow-up, in turn, is the task suited for the detective. She or he wants to make sure all the facts are on the table – both during and after the interview.

The opening of the interview is important. Establish the atmosphere. If you're trying to take the edge off, some experts advocate admitting you are nervous. We suggest cracking a joke, talking about the weather or hobbies, commenting on the office you are in, or something else relatively lighthearted.

As we were walking into the room at the beginning of our interview with the CEO of a large industrial corporation, we overheard the CEO and his secretary discussing the weather – and whether it was appropriate for repairing his sailing boat. We quickly hooked on to this conversation as we passed through the secretary's room and into the CEO's office. We started talking about the joy of sailing and about how relaxing it must be to work outdoors, getting away from the hectic life in the office. This won his appeal, and both of us were at ease from that point forward. Two-thirds into the interview, we felt confident enough to raise critical questions about his role in the corporation. This also went OK, mostly because his mind was still wandering to his sailboat. The lesson: Find your interviewee's nirvana – take him there. Only then can you do what you came for.

The interview situation calls for confidence, calmness, and control -- and also for improvisation. The Norwegian journalist Steinfeld, whose interview skills we cited earlier, says he improvises during an interview as a rule, rather than the exception. The way you improvise depends on your personality, experience, and also on your current state of mind. Are you confident? Are you rested and calm -- or eager, stressed, and nervous? Interview expert Grant McCracken says you need to use yourself as an instrument in the research process. Play the strings you feel most comfortable with. Feminist scholar Ann Oakley goes even further. She claims the interviewer must be prepared to invest his or her own personal identity in the relationship. This implies giving personal accounts and examples from your own life, offering empathy. You may also have to admit weakness.

The interview challenges you, and it challenges the person you are interviewing. You need to be on the edge, risking that your questions are perceived as naïve. You are not having a group discussion. Dealing with your own frustrations in this regard is justified, but avoid communicating your own point of view, as it could block the process. You need to be provocative; to inspire disclosure; to stimulate discussion, reflection, and interest. You need to demonstrate that you find his or her thoughts on this issue important.

What kind of competence should you display when interviewing the elite? Should you come across as knowledgeable? Interview experts usually say you should not come across as stupid but, certainly, not claim to know it all. Most interview textbooks claim you should pretend you do not know anything about the issue at hand. You should open up, allowing others to use their own words. Actually, in our experience, the opposite is true. The elite resist interviewers who possess little or no subject knowledge. In fact, it is better to show off some of your knowledge in order to gain some credibility.

American social scientists Jean Lave and Etienne Wenger argues that legitimate peripheral participation (i.e., you are present and accepted but have limited responsibility, maybe only carrying out routine tasks) is very important to learning. Day-today observation of best practices, they say, is the best way to learn any trade.

There is always a community in which you are an apprentice, even as the CEO of a company. You should take this attitude when visiting any of the departments and teams with which you liaise. Know where to find it and know what role you fall into. For instance, if you are a public affairs professional, your network of colleagues will always include people with more experience. Learn from them; get inspired and grow from their experiences.

Now back to the interview position itself. The interview is a reflective process during which your informant might learn as much as you. According to Norwegian feminist scholar Merete Lie, a good interviewer participates in the reflection process.

In conclusion, access is a precarious, ongoing, bargaining process. Inside connections, persistence, social skills, and improvisation are all important. Trust, respect, reciprocity, professional prestige, and even self-esteem come into play. Human encounters cannot and should not be completely planned out.

With recent advances in technology, gaining access has at once become both easier and more difficult. Access is easier, because new access points, like e-mail and online communities, have evolved. Access is more difficult because the powerful always find ways to protect their time – using those same tools. What works will depend upon the setting. Success will also depend on your mindset – whether you are able to shift between the journalistic, therapeutic, and investigative modi operandi.

Leadership from below is about maximizing your own powers. Work in more subtle, egalitarian ways. Focus on delivering what the other person wants, needs, or appreciates. Give a little, and receive more.

Leadership from below	Lesson #4
You get maximum access to people, networks, and trends when you alternate between the journalistic, therapeutic, and investigative mindsets. Leadership is built through relationships.	

Chapter 5

Performing in front of people

Performance does not occur in isolation. Leaders are comfortable in all social situations – encounters, ceremonies, meetings, teams, projects. They master the whole spectrum of daily life as a professional. With the right exposure, awareness, and training, everyone can reach such mastery.

J ohn F. Kennedy was full of self-confidence when confronted with people. Whether one on one, in a crowd, or in a televised debate, he always seemed to know what to say and how to behave. He was a grounded leader and a people person. But he had also been carefully groomed from childhood.

Most of us are not that fortunate. And, luckily, we do not compete with Kennedy.

While teams are important, there are other demanding social situations that a leader must handle. In fact, leadership from below can be seen as a series of social situations: the serendipitous encounter, the interview, the meeting, the team, the ceremony, and the presentation.

The prepared encounter

The brief encounter is ideal if you have a quick heads-up, a lead, or a chance to influence a decision – without having to take too much time out of your own agenda. Not all leaders know how to arrange such "spontaneous" encounters, but Kennedy did. To others, it seemed like every moment was such a moment.

"All relationships of people to each other rest, as a matter of course, upon the precondition that they know something about each other"
– Georg Simmel

How do you increase the probability of encounters? Good encounters can occur in transient places: in hallways, elevators, lunch queues, and subways, or on the street outside an office building. Catching people outside their own context, and still outside yours, works well. Nobody has a territory to defend. To be a leader of encounters is easy: Be around, be approachable, take the initiative, and award the same behavior in others.

Ceremonies

What, exactly, is a ceremony? The other day, Julie, an administrative assistant I know, sent an email about a colleague's upcoming birthday. The previous week, she mentioned that there were chocolates up for grabs in another colleague's office. These emails were not strictly informational; they were hints about ceremonial elements of the workplace -- locations where people relax, build friendships, and learn helpful tips.

Leaders show up to such things, even when less busy people do not. Ceremonies in the workplace serve to inspire, reward excellence, and celebrate group accomplishments.

Many social occasions have ceremonial elements. But beware the regular meeting that becomes a ceremony to reassure the boss of his powers. Make sure that boss is not you. The meeting-turned-ceremony is characterized by hierarchical command structure, with each individual reporting to and looking directly at the boss, not the group; the boss's final conclusions do not necessarily reflect what was said. Most regularly scheduled meetings, daily or weekly, have some of these features.

I have had the misfortune of taking part in such a weekly meeting for two years. Individuals who spoke in that meeting addressed only the boss, and there was no discussion within the group itself. Over time, group spirit disintegrated, and the majority of the group regarded the meeting as a waste of time; 30 people "wasted" two and a half hours a week.

Leaders avoid such meetings, cut them short, leave early, or make the most of them -- capitalizing on the format to spread rapid messages beyond the agenda. However, if you are caught in a meeting like this, you can still speak up and flag a few high-level issues. You can chat to people you rarely see before or after the meeting, or try to catch the boss. You can bring outside reading material. Or you can meditate. Do not be paralyzed; there are many ways to make this time productive.

Meetings

Meetings are convenient if they are regular and brief, ad hoc and brief, or democratic and brief. In short, if they do not drag on. Like many firms, Xerox, the American document management company, has guidelines for maintaining high-quality meetings.[19] However, most leaders naturally contribute to effective meetings, regardless of company policy.

Before the meeting, be sure to introduce people to each other, or introduce the leader. Be aware that the role of facilitator is a powerful one. Talkers waste time and are easily recognized in any group. They must be marginalized, or you lose time. Ask about the agenda early on. If the agenda is unclear, take a minute to restate it in your own words. Speak up to give your own view of the meeting and what it should accomplish. In fact, don't waste your time going to a meeting without speaking to the group. Take control of your own outcome (which is not necessarily the meeting's outcome).

Meetings can take many forms. Ensure that they make all participants feel welcome, competent, and confident. Keep an optimistic tone. Create a good atmosphere, maybe with a funny observation. You want people to share, but not too much. Ask a question, but only if it clarifies or deepens the discussion. You do not want to take too much room. Allow others to speak -- mostly listen -- especially if you are not put in charge.

Fred, 56, a director in the public sector, always interrupts. Nobody except for Fred has the opportunity to finish a sentence. He always tells his subordinates, "You should work faster"; "You should work better than this, I mean"; "Prepare these things" – regardless of how much you have prepared. He usually overturns established protocol and has been known to take charge of a meeting he was not already chairing. In short, he is the epitome of an office bully. The only two strategies to effectively combat this behavior are to (1) to keep silent; or (2) agree with everything he says. Leaders from below, just stay low.

Leaders should be aware that knowledge workers do not really like being in meetings and avoid them if possible. Generation Y workers, born between 1970 and 1990, are especially impatient. Rather than boycotting meetings, the smart thing to do is to make them short and efficient. Resolve issues, share problems, and focus on upcoming challenges.

Leaders avoid meetings that drag on. You may even leave the meeting before it is over, although that is risky. You save a great deal of frustration, but you miss the sweet ending. The wrap-up is an opportunity for you to get a last word in. The vacuum that develops immediately after the meeting is a good time to talk to your boss or whomever you need to involve in your next project. If you are quick, you will always have your say, even with people two or three steps above you in the hierarchy: They will assume you are fascinated by something they said. Just repeat their main message and say you agree. Then, get on with your issue, and move on.

Conferences

Conferences give you the opportunity to meet between 100 and 10,000 people, depending on their size and your skill set. Now, the utility also depends on the potential of those same people. But assuming that you choose your venues carefully, a conference is a tremendously rich opportunity. My wife and I met at a conference, so we are impartial to such arenas as a source of moments of wisdom.

As a leader you spend a great deal of time organizing, attending, or reporting from workshops, seminars, and conferences. If you gain a reputation as someone with organizational skills, you will be asked to lead workshops and to invite people of your choosing to advance an agenda. That is an effective way to gain access to new networks and to the knowledge that can put you ahead of the crowd.

"A man is well educated when he knows where to find what he doesn't know" – Georg Simmel

There is also an art to conference behavior. You must know how to filter the agenda to attend only the promising presentations. Rapidly assess whether you are in the right place. Always sit at the edge of the room, toward the back, so you can make a quick exit if needed. Make the most of all the social encounters possible between and even during meetings. An alternative strategy is to sit close to people you want to speak with or get to know. From the front, you can't see the audience, and you waste your time looking at the canvas or the speaker. Most people do not go to conferences to listen to speeches but, rather, spend most of their time scouting the room, looking for customers, contacts, and clues to future trends relevant to their organization or professional development. Leaders sit toward the back or on the side, with a clear view of as many people as possible.

After a conference, you must assess. Follow up with the people you met. Connect with them on LinkedIn or other non-intrusive professional communities. Send an email. Arrange to meet or speak with them again. Without such follow-up, momentum is lost.

Organizations

To be in an organization means taking part in the most stable of all social situations in the contemporary work setting. In all likelihood, you seldom reflect on what that means. If you work in one, chances are, there are established ways of doing things that ensure a certain coherence and consistency among employees. Without such a performance culture, there is no way to differentiate one organization from the other.

Management consulting firms are in the business of selling. What they sell and discuss is a method -- their own way of dealing with business challenges. What consultants do is seldom different; they endeavor to be perceived as unique, but their method is always process improvement. We all know that no two organizations are the same. Learn to recognize whom you're dealing with and whom you work for.

Summing up, know where to be; plan; have a strategy on location. Make the most of your presence – or stay home. Your organization is only a small part of your professional life. The average person has up to ten different employers during her professional career -- and far more positions within one company. The only constants are your network and yourself. Those are the elements you have to work with.

Leadership from below	Lesson #5
Leaders who successfully navigate the spectrum of professional situations have a powerful impact also beyond the organization they work for.	

Chapter 6

From "me" to "we"

While teams can be an effective way to organize, not all teams are effective. Leadership is always a shared commodity in a team, since nobody fully controls a team process. While discipline is crucial, if you want to succeed, social aspects cannot be overlooked.

Team members share roles and responsibilities crucial to their task's success. In one project, you may be the formal leader but depend on others for key insights. In another project, you watch others excel but may have unique experience in a vital area. If you are very outspoken, you can rally people to support you when there is time to make a decision. You may be the social leader in the group. The important thing: You must think and lead simultaneously.

In the last decade, business has been seen rapid innovation. Those who fail to innovate die -- unless they operate a monopoly. (And eventually, monopolies also die, due to government regulations or because an ever-changing business environment.) Innovation grows in importance. Fresh perspectives are held in high regard but cannot possibly come from the insiders alone. And while insiders are important, one person alone cannot change much. What matters: Look around yourself, and work with what you have. Within any organization, there are insiders and outsiders. A team has a great deal of knowledge that is inaccessible those not on the team. This holds true even for colleagues who have been part of a company for 20 years.

Jon R. Katzenbach and Douglas K. Smith's 1993 classic *The Wisdom of Teams* posits that corporate teams must be small, diverse, and accountable. Their follow up tome, 2001's *The Discipline of Teams*, indicated that successful teams depend not so much on bonding, togetherness, and empowerment but, rather, on discipline -- all of which is true. But there is more: Meetings, for instance, must be issue-driven. You have to allow time to solve the issue. Do not stick strictly to project plans. Effective teams, wrote Katzenbach and Smith, alternate leaders even when completing one task. All members are mutually accountable.

A Hollywood soundstage or a large public-sector consulting project, are both examples of team settings. A team is a small group of people, usually twelve or less, working together for a limited time to achieve common goals. If the team is larger, additional people perform marginal roles or act as subcontractors to the main delivery. A successful team is a group whose elements (e.g., people, process, leadership, and resources) lead to deliveries that match or exceed initial expectations.

Teams command a set of resources and are affected by several factors specific to their task, the individuals on their team, the setting, and the sector. Other factors may intervene.

Successful teams believe in their task and command sufficient resources to reach their goal. They have a social leader, as well as a task leader (neither of which may be the assigned project leader), and they spend considerable time face to face. When forced to meet online, they are aware of the current limitations; communicate carefully and do not spend too much time on controversial issues.

The bulk of existing research on teams indicates that while all teams are working on a task or task, most teams devote equal time to maintaining the social relationships within the team.[20]

Teams differ in degree of complexity, and you need to know which factors come into play in your own team. Even more importantly, as we will see, every team must become a "we" before anything useful can happen.

Clarify the task – ask the obvious questions

On September 11, 2001, when U.S. Vice President Richard B. Cheney convened a meeting in the secure command center under the White House, no one invited to the meeting knew the meeting's purpose -- or what to do. Subsequently, many questioned whether the right team members were present. But the people who showed up were forced to act as if they were a team. This is relatively common, although often in less extreme circumstances. No team knows exactly what they are supposed to be doing from the outset. That is a big problem. Past experience does not always dictate what to do about it either: Teams differ; expectations differ;

constraints differ. Whether you lead a team or are just a member of one, make sure that you clarify the team's task. Variables include time, clarity, realism of the goal and purpose, budget, resources, and allotted staff time.

Once I led a team tasked with creating a new, green technology policy for the Kingdom of Norway. We lost several weeks in empty discussions due to lack of clarity. I initially thought the task and mandate was clear. I later learned that, while it was clear to me, I did not make it clear to the rest of the team. We each brought different ideas and different agendas. To some, "green" was not the same as "environmentally friendly." To another subset, promoting electric transport was a good thing; to others, it was a just one part of a much larger picture. To some, increasing reliance on nuclear power signaled impending Armageddon; to others, it was a divine solution.

Also, the team's focus evolved throughout the project. Poorly compensated team members reacted differently. Some were confused and lost motivation due to lack of clarity. Others saw their involvement as an opportunity and seized it, trying to communicate their economic or ideological interests.

A leader will always clarify the task at the outset, whether he is assigned to lead the team, becomes the de facto team leader, or works as a member of the team: Write down the task in simple language; show it to the team; discuss it; and ensure that everyone more or less agrees, including the team and the customer. All of this should happen by the end of the team's first face-to-face meeting. If necessary, it can be revised later; by then, you know what is expected. Make sure that all unclear issues are discussed up front. Do not cut short this discussion, as that could lead to problems later.

Recently, I led the launch of a website and online community for a major European actor. The target community was 100,000 people. Six months into the project, we were still briefing the consulting firm team on the basic tasks required by the project. Communicating the main message is crucial to the success of the project. With new members joining the team every month, repetition and clear messages are fundamental. I did not realize this at the outset, as things were clear in the contract and kick-off memorandum – to which no one refers once the project is underway.

Talk to people right away

When leaders join a team, the first task is to cultivate allies. Without support, we will not convince anyone of our viewpoints and ideas. Start by assessing whom you need to work with, and move on.

Teams comprise individuals; even if they all work in your organization or have the same background, each team member is different. On or immediately subsequent to Day 1, talk to all team members individually. Establishing personal rapport is always better than an introduction in a group setting. For example, when starting a new job, I arrived early for a unit meeting that was to be attended by 30 people. One other employee arrived just as early as I did, which gave us the opportunity to get to know each other before the meeting commenced. For the next six months, she was an ally, spreading good news about me – which was a miracle, because the co-worker was a bully and left the unit one year later.

A good team has a set of composite skills that match the task. This includes some intrinsic diversity that may or may not contribute to the innovation needed to succeed. At the outset, you will not necessarily know what these skills are, but it is important to have a competent team with a diverse skills base: A set of people who can draw from very different experiences will enhance creativity and ensures greater technical competence. But a common reference point is required -- a working style or mentality that holds the work together. If you are not, as a matter of habit, taking note as to whether this is the case, start doing so whenever you enter a room and are expected to work with teammates. Similarly, you can start looking for allies -- people who can support you in your own agenda. Develop a good rapport with them right away. It will save time and give you an advantage over non-leaders.

From "me" to "us" - the effect of telling a joke

Jerry Seinfeld's four levels of comedy are: *"Make your friends laugh; make strangers laugh; get paid to make strangers laugh; and make people talk like you, because it's so much fun."* Leaders would do well in following that recipe.

A group of individuals do not become a team just because you call them a team and give them a task. Have you ever joined a team in which no one introduced you, yet you went straight to work? Chances are, it did not work very well -- or it took you longer to get involved.

Once you have conducted your initial assessment of the individuals around you, start thinking of how the team itself will function. What is the most effective role for you to play? Where will your skills and experience be best utilized?

Teams come in all shapes. Key team variables are team composition, location, allegiances, unspoken issues, mood, previous history, team process, discussion climate, skills, informal and formal relations, leadership, communication, power dynamics, leadership, common ground, meaning and belonging, uniqueness of team, and sustainability. We are not going to go through all of that – teams are far more complex than a small book can handle.

Leadership from below means taking charge of a team as if you were the one responsible for its result, regardless of what mandate you are given. Teams always have informal leaders. Make sure you bid for that position. But if others do as well, find your role without making too much of a fuss. You may have a more fruitful role as the devil's advocate, an emotional leader, a deal-maker at decision time, or an expert who remains on the sidelines while monitoring the team's needs.

Grasp the setting quickly

The expression the "First 100 days" was first used by Franklin D. Roosevelt, thirty-second president of the United States, requesting a grace period for the New Deal to work before it was quashed. Nowadays, most leaders have 100 days (or is it 100 minutes?) before criticism arises. So you must quickly grasp the setting. People are, rightly so, impatient. Why are you in charge? What do you offer?

Nothing matters more to a leader than figuring out the situation and the setting. What is the context of this work assignment? What is the organizational framework? What are the performance metrics? To what degree is there management buy-in for what has to be done? What are the beneficiary/customer demands? How much face-to-face contact can you invest? How is the situation perceived by stakeholders or outsiders?

Settings can vary enormously. One reason why management advice fails is that it is applied in an evolving, novel setting, where new factors come into play. Always analyze a setting carefully. Consult others. Then decide on your approach. You may want to influence the setting slightly, change some parameters, or ask for more or fewer resources. Finally, you should improvise – take the things proven to a success in one setting, and apply it to another. Proceed with care.

Working Successfully with Teams[21]

Regardless of how much you know, not all your teams will succeed. But there are some basics. All teams try to take care of two things at once: maintaining their own cohesion and addressing the task at hand. The former is fairly straightforward: You need to maintain a good relationship with team members. The latter also seems obvious, since no team is together without a task. The task may vary in clarity, but common factors will include some idea of what work has to be done, what resources are available, to whom it will be delivered, and in what timeframe. Most importantly, the team is the sum of the members -- not you as the leader. The math is easy: You are one person, and you will always be outnumbered by your team members. Leaders from below are mindful of the mathematical perspective of their own importance. Your team members will appreciate this and be more motivated as a result. And with greater motivation, the results will follow.

The virtual team

Virtual teams are common in today's global industry. Oftentimes, virtual teams are formed ad hoc, which makes sense, given the lack of travel time and the high cost of travel. Other times, it's company strategy. Experiences are seldom documented, but some evidence exists:[22] The Institute of Cultural Affairs is a non-profit with offices in 30 countries. They seldom meet but maintain unity through a common aim and some common activities. Trying to resolve conflicts over the phone or by email is tricky and time-consuming. Misunderstandings are a frequent occurrence and take time to resolve.

Meeting in person is too expensive, but otherwise all offices realize its benefit.

The reality of the contemporary workplace is that most teams are hybrids – working online and offline concurrently. Even co-located teams may work largely over email, to the extent that many co-located workers seldom meet face to face. However, the degree to which one relies on virtual communications is situation-specific. In the aftermath of the September 11 attacks, increased security within the White House complex became increasingly time-consuming. People would meet in cafés outside the office environment to work more efficiently by email and telephone. Whatever you do, spend enough time face to face. Only then can you achieve the full effect of virtual collaboration.

The team – solving problems and dealing with dissent

The team is the core of knowledge work. Dealing with dissent is difficult. It is also important. People will disagree. Watch for the rules in place to regulate it. If there are none, suggest some. Most teams get along well with a few rules that are established at the beginning (e.g., when to employ majority rule and when to use unanimity). In principle, it is best to let team members feel as though they have decided the rules. Rules should emerge from the discussion during the first meeting.

I once had to assemble an independent group of experts to assess a policy challenge[23] -- no easy task. There are always constraints and complex issues to consider. First of all, experts are rarely paid well. I appeal to their sense of public duty. In the groups I put together, I ended up with between seven and ten experts, assuming that too many would slow down the work. They were from a spectrum of fields and sectors – professors, scientists, social scientists, and industry professionals. I planned to have eight meetings over one year. The aim was to publish a report, hold a hearing, and issue a short newsletter to the government.

Surprisingly, the team members spent about two months molding themselves into a team. The first meeting was deceivingly successful: nearly 100 percent attendance, smiling faces, and so many impressive CVs around the same table. However, in a managerial capacity, we forgot to clearly spell out expectations. Also, the discussion around the mandated and expected outcomes was cut short. Now, after the fact, it all seems so clear.

A year later, when writing the final report, a great deal of time was spent discussing the role of this report in the public debate. I spent a lot of time doing the team members' work, as they were suddenly too busy to write or even to show up. Stipulating a clear commitment on Day 1 may have reduced the team by one or two members but, in the end, produced a more fruitful outcome. The lesson: Never sacrifice project output to a happy-go -lucky kick-off that you cannot sustain.

Leadership from below	Lesson #6
Leaders work well in teams, taking on key roles where they see fit. Successful leaders match the challenges before them by being task-focused and aware of team dynamics, evolving from "me" to "we."	

Chapter 7

Mastering mobility

As technology advances, people are more mobile than before, and information loads increase. Yet some things remain the same: Distance always matters. How to travel?

Futurists will have it that there is so much information available in today's world that a new kind of leader must emerge: a superhuman who is increasingly capable of selecting what to focus on. True, but human imagination has always been infinite, and comparisons to the past are difficult to make. Who is to say, for instance, that it was easier to be a successful merchant in Renaissance Venice than to be a leader in the year 2008?

My grandfather Per was a Protestant European missionary who spent seven years in Madagascar, the immense island on the eastern coast of Africa. During World War II, his family spent three months on a boat bound for home, crossing the Cape of Good Hope, only to be stranded in South Africa for months. Rather than enduring five years of German occupation of his native Norway, he was on Africa's tip, waiting for things to calm down. His knowledge was hard-earned. He was awarded the pleasure of spending the next ten years giving speeches to churches north of the Polar circle, often sleeping in unheated homes and seeing his family only once every two months. Per's story illustrates why it is essential to sift through a great number of impressions in order to function most effectively. Who is to say that the laborers of the past were not superior to today's workers at the task of focusing on what is most important?

And what is different today? The main drivers of knowledge work are the previously mentioned globalization flows that impact the degree of distance between customers, suppliers, and co-workers -- especially relevant are the flows of technology, people, and culture.

The *impact of technology*: the Internet, as well as innovative, larger, more, cheaper, or better transport technologies and infrastructures (e.g., airplanes, global airport network, trains, cars, and buses). The growth, spread, and uptake are relevant for technology's impact on our *mobility patterns*. More people travel farther, to new places, across borders. In so doing, minds, mouths, and moods meet.

As a consequence, a *melting pot of cultural mentalities* is constantly evolving. New organizational ideas and theories – such as the nomadic vision of work anywhere, anytime – or the interplay of traditional, modern, and immigrant cultures as we see in Bangalore, New York, etc. The global melting pot is not the only result. Resistance develops when people's basic needs are not met, protests are not heard, and ideas are not allowed to blossom.

However, among globally winning trends, the *emergence of egalitarian leaders and entrepreneurship* is quite new. Scores of new leaders are bred as we speak. Leaders will play a role in reshaping society because they are motivated to do so and because they have backing from the people.

In 2009, there will be 850 million global mobile workers, up from 650 million in 2004, according to global market intelligence firm IDC. This is a tremendous increase, especially since most of these workers are concentrated in the urban areas of the 30 well-to-do Organisation for Economic Co-operation and Development (OECD) countries. The main drivers of mobility are changing work patterns, business structures, and collaboration styles.

Public-private partnerships contribute to shattering the notion that work can occur in one location only. Companies launch larger and larger projects, engage in multi-disciplinary teams, and develop complex systems. Coordination of such large systems is also difficult and entails collaboration often across Oceans. Mergers and takeovers mean that people increasingly work with others across sites, and keep changing teammates and colleagues. New technology enables advanced modeling using digital mock-ups. Designs can be shared across the Internet. Companies use less office space – since workers do not spend their time in the office anyway. Finally, reducing the carbon footprint is another reason why firms choose to hold virtual meetings or team processes.

Moving is not always desirable, and it's a major source of tension. For that reason, many experiment with working virtually. However, while the initial visions of mobile work forecasted tremendous and immediate changes in the way work was conducted, it has taken some time. Thirty years on, the revolution is not over. What started in the years after World War II, with advances in travel technology and infrastructure (e.g., airports and highways), continues today. The usage patterns have been difficult to predict. In the 1960s, American futurists claimed that the financial and economic elites would dominate as mobile professionals. In contrast, throughout the 1970s and 1980s, software programmers and academics in the Western world continued to be pioneer users. When mobility and supporting technologies became more common, many were surprised to discover that the pool of mobile workers in the United States not only comprised C-level executives, but also managers, sales staff, consultants, and support technicians – the middle classes.

As we move into the next decade, students, the elderly (who live longer than ever before), and even children are new markets for mobility. Independence from place gradually increases. There are now more cell phones in Asia than in any other part of the world. In some African countries, telephone lines are nonexistent, but the cell phone is available to even the very poor. Some of this is due to the intervention of donor aid agencies. In other instances, it is simply the result of market forces.

A mobile work style[24]

Mobility is always relative to your profession, and also to the situation. One week you may be stuck in one location, fixing a problem, helping out with family matters in your hometown, or taking part in a team process. Another week, you may move around constantly, traveling between multiple sites visiting customers, suppliers, or R&D labs. The important thing: Be where it matters the most at any given time.

When the idea of the working nomad emerged in the late 1990s, there were many advertisements depicting people working in hotels, airports, trains, buses, and the like. The truth of the matter is that while you may indeed get something done in these transient spaces, they do not dominate your working time.

There is actually good reason not to work in an environment where people run around, where there are other activities competing for your attention – shopping, communicating, resting, or just winding down and thinking. Early on, those aspects of a knowledge worker's life were under played, probably because the phenomenon was so new, and advertisers were trying to capitalize on what they thought was a completely new lifestyle. Also, the pioneer users had been computer programmers and researchers -- groups with exceptional concentration ability and interest in technology. They tend to spend all their energy on the current problem at hand.

"Find your own work style, know when to isolate yourself and when to be social, when to listen and when to present your ideas"

When the more diverse business crowd became mobile nomads, marketers at first assumed they would spend all their waking time on the computer, also hard at work. Most of them did not. In fact, knowledge work was and is so much more than typing on a computer. Nowadays, with mobility going mainstream, we are beginning to understand that work is a complex activity that can't be broken down into its essential components. We do yet not know exactly what people do, when they work, and why. Work is, in fact, a remarkably misunderstood activity.

Leaders must find themselves able to mix and match working style to the surroundings; it is a constant activity. The most important types of mobile work modes are: micro-mobility, temporary mobility, pendulum mobility, and network mobility.

The micro-mobile mode is when you work mostly in one place but move around inside that location, with a walking radius of fewer than 15 minutes. You have almost instant access to your entire workspace. Some examples of people who do this often are office workers, teachers, airport personnel, and hospital-based doctors.

In temporarily mobile mode, you are mainly located in an office. Occasionally, you work away from your fixed location but only in other temporary workplaces. Professions that make house calls, such as social workers are temporarily mobile. Likewise, workers who travel, commute, or respond to emergency situations (e.g., firefighters, police, etc.) or those who execute maintenance tasks on customer premises (e.g., computer repair technicians, plumbers, janitors, gardeners, electricians, and cleaning staff) are temporarily mobile.

Pendulum mobile people alternate between working in two fixed locations, such as home and work. The classical teleworker, popular since the late 1980s, falls in this category. Today, only self-employed or short-term contract agents are truly pendulum mobile, because most tasks require intense consultation with markets, stakeholders, and clients, with a larger geographic spread.

People who are moving from one location to another all the time have nomadic work modes (e.g., sales staff, managers frequently reassigned to new project sites, and consultants). C-level executives at Fortune 500 companies often travel internationally between a myriad of corporate office locations, to conferences and customer meetings. Crossing time zones creates a host of other issues related to sleep, culture, language, infrastructure, time, cost, and the inability to work simultaneously. On the other hand, in the

United States, there are many professionals working for smaller firms who spend an equivalent number of days on the road, traveling locally, regionally, or nationally. When you work within the same country, receiving generally uniform impressions from your work locations, travel is less disruptive.

People who are on the move -- transporting goods, people, or information between nodes -- are in network mode. Increasingly, they are also e-enabled. People carry with them advanced applications that provide location- or context-sensitive information. Emergency staff, transporters, truck drivers, cab drivers, and pilots are examples. Leaders tend to find their preferred mobility mode by experimenting.

Learn when to move around and when to stay in place. These choices are made daily, even hourly. Work from home if you need to balance time between work, leisure and family. Work on location, with a client, or show up for a meeting if there likely is a decision being made. Spend your face-to-face time where it matters the most. Don't waste valuable proximity on the computer, in one-to-many communication (unless you are doing the talking), or on tasks you could do alone: interact, confront, inspire.

The technology of mobile work

Mobile work requires an elaborate social and economic infrastructure: You need physical networks of roads, highways, cities, airports, and train stations planned wisely and with adequate facilities for expansion. The challenge of matching these structures with the adequate amount and appropriate kinds of cars, planes, trains, and buses is not met, and network mobile leaders suffer the most.

While the postal system was the first groundbreaking mobile communication system, the fax was its digital sister. Faxing was invented by Alexander Bain, a Scottish mechanic who, in 1843, received a British patent. However, the fax did not gain currency until the 1970s, due to the cost of the underlying technology and the needs of modern business practices. In fact, the Telecopier, invented by Xerox in 1966, became the first successful facsimile machine. However, once it gained momentum, the exponential increase in value of each fax machine for each important user became immediately apparent. The network logic was in motion. The fax will survive until digital signature is fully available in offices everywhere, which may happen sometime in the next decade or so.

The telephone took a long time to settle in society. Sociologist Claude Fischer's work on the social history of the telephone illustrates how, in the beginning, everyone thought the phone would be used only by business. However, even in the first decade of the telephone, it was a social tool. The first phones were installed on farm fields but were not used solely to discuss crop yields and communicate transport needs. Farmers and farm workers talked to their families across great distances, as they were often migrant workers. Private homes installed telephones to talk to family and friends from a distance. Businesses were slower to catch on.

In addition to the telephone, the fax, and the pager, the landmark invention that developed stepwise between 1970 and 2000 was the Internet. None of these technologies developed automatically. These were either accidental discoveries, incremental innovation based on market developments, or the fruit of national infrastructure policies. In the 1970s, the U.S. funding of the Defense Advanced Research Project Agency (DARPA) led to an earlier version of the Internet (Arpanet) and secured America's early dominance of domains. Neither entrepreneurship nor inevitable technological progress played a significant part in this early phase; serendipity ruled. However, when there was a technological chain in motion, momentum kicked in.

"There is always, at any given time, a maximum ideal distance between co-workers"

The future of technology

Amid such a period of growth and amazing changes, one may assume that the trend will continue. If so, we will not even recognize the world in a decade. Will technologies continue to enable more and more virtual work? There are certainly some constraining factors, such as environment, distance, and resources:

Distance will always matter. There is always, at any given time, a maximum ideal distance between co-workers. Even though this distance has increased with the opportunities of new technology, proximity is always superior, because it provides the richest communication. Body language combines with a common physical environment with which you can interact and bring into the conversation Further, technology always enhances proximity and vice versa. Even if, one day, great technology combines with co-presence, technology alone will never win the race. During meetings, position yourself at the center of the most communication. Distance will matter, but more and better work will be conducted across ever greater distances. Leadership from below means taking this into account.

Cost will always matter. We will get more advanced, but everything will always have a cost. Cost/benefit will therefore always be an issue. The Internet was never free. In fact, free riding was only ever possible for a decade or so. Even so, someone was always paying. Governments and firms paid for the infrastructure. Companies tried to get customers hooked by giving away freebies like surfing, temporarily low roaming fees (what a feast that was!), free shipping, etc. Information has a price. Knowledge, on the other hand, is almost priceless; its value literally cannot be measured.

People will always matter. Computers and networks have enabled a great deal of progress, but even knowledge workers at high-tech firms need to meet face to face sometimes. If you try to pitch project ideas, gain consensus, and shift momentum away from the people who matter, you fail. When in crisis or when in need of heavy discussion, fly to meet your opponent face-to-face. The importance of meeting people is not likely to diminish.

The environment will always matter. The environment is at the same time a barrier and an enabler of less travel. If we travel less, there is less strain on the environment. If we travel more, we see more of nature's variety and experience a wider spectrum of human contact. Regardless, given the vital focus on our carbon footprint, the environment will impact knowledge work in the foreseeable future.

Leadership from below	Lesson #7
Distance always matters. By all means, find your own working style and move around. But always be where it matters the most.	

Chapter 8

Taking charge of your senses

Leaders need to make full use of sense perception, which entails becoming more aware of body language, touch, taste, and eyesight. Savvy leaders reap huge benefits from sense awareness, because it brings you closer to people around you, professionally and at home.

Investor Dan could have sat in an office on the top floor of a huge building with doormen, secretaries, and assistants protecting him. In fact, there are two perfect locations in Northern California for someone like him: the financial district in San Francisco or Sand Hill Road in Palo Alto, where all the big investment firms are. Instead, Dan chooses to run between a college campus and a small, two-story building in Berkeley, constantly sweating on behalf of his seed investments, talking to them all the time, arranging meetings, and doing day-to-day coaching.

The offices of Incubator Inc. are located in a small building not very far from the University of California campus. As the boss, Dan maintains close relations with university graduates (he has spent considerable time at the university) and knows many venture capitalists. A graduate of the university's Haas School of Business, Dan says professors pass along to him most of Incubator Inc.'s deal flow. Dan's relations are primarily with the Computer Science and Business Departments. Dan enjoys working with students and spends a great deal of time speaking at student events. When I spoke with him, he had lectured on campus the previous week. About 10 percent of his profits are donated back to the university. Dan works with four new teams every year and makes an average of seven deals a year; the average company stays six months in the business incubator, receiving his full attention.

"My place is like an old, sweaty gym," he says. "It consists very much of day-to-day work." And what does Dan do? He gives intense, daily attention to his companies, takes care of the space, handles some of the customer relations, and seeks "bridge" financing. Incubators are a funnel for venture capitalists. Angel investors do it to spread risk, says Dan.

One of his companies is GetOutdoors.com, a portal for bicycles, boats, and other outdoor products. The young entrepreneurs wanted to finance their venture with banner advertising, and direct retail. Since they arrived at Incubator Inc., Dan has suggested several strategic changes to their business concept. Now, he says they are more like the CNET of the outdoors. CNET is the major portal for technology products (tagline: "the source of computers and technology"). GetOutdoors.com now boasts "everything needed to go outdoors" -- and a completely refurbished business model. The start-up no longer aims to take on the whole logistic processes of existing retailers but, rather, to act as a middleman. Dan's insider knowledge in the high-tech marketplace proves crucial to young entrepreneurs who come right out of university. His contacts and close contact with the market helps them to build momentum and take part in Silicon Valley placemaking. Entrepreneurship is a quality of effective knowledge workers.

Watching for strategic change on a day-to-day basis is part of the job. It means to take care of whatever the business needs at the time, whether small or large. Dan has good relations with Berkeley lawyers. "A lawyer is a gateway to investors and all sorts of clients," he explains. In fact, so important are these relationships that you cannot be without them. You have to be part of the buzz. Always be out there, and attend plenty of forums." For example, you can join *Fast Company* magazine's "Company of Friends," a global reader's network.

Dan provides a service that is place-bound. He spends most of his time on the phone trying to secure the interest of venture capitalists, setting up meetings with them, and in strategy sessions with his companies. He would not dream of doing this elsewhere. This is where he knows his way around. This is where he has his contacts – both supply and demand (lawyers, investors, advisors, professors, graduates, students, etc.). Berkeley is his playground, his little place in the New Economy. It is a niche few can beat right now (I visited Dan in 2001). Berkeley is small. You can get to most parts of the town without entering one of the many highways that penetrate the outskirts of the city. The proximity, combined with a complex cultural environment of "shared understanding" dating back to the 1960s, provides the emotional glue. But work practices are also situated in pragmatic decisions about how to be the most efficient in your daily workday

Dan embodies the principles of Leadership from below: He is modest; he levels with his employees; and he helps where needed. Most importantly, he is there.

Dan's story illustrates what Chicago sociologist Saskia Sassen (1994) has argued about financial districts – they are place-bound because of the fragile processes of creating trust. Convincing work needs face-to-face contact, even to make sense of face-to-screen investments. What exactly drives this need for being in physical proximity? What do offline skills entail? With our technological fascination, we risk losing the edge of effective body language, active use of sense perception and intuition, and, ultimately, miss out on the power of personal charisma.

"The five basic senses – hearing, sight, smell, taste, and touch – are still far too advanced to be successfully transmitted by today's technology"

Build body language

Shouting at people, putting your arm around someone – our bodies are active when we try to convince people and to forcefully communicate our point. The importance of body language in the workplace[25] is not easy to describe with words alone. Better said, you must feel the difference.

Leadership from below principles teaches you to respect others in the way you move your body -- and to use extreme language only when needed. The way you stand, sit, gesticulate, and speak has an effect on your boss, your co-workers, and your audience. But exactly how it works is difficult to know. One boss told me: "I am not sure whether you were upset with me earlier. I did not feel you supported me in that meeting." Yet we had not uttered a word during the meeting. But we might have forgotten to nod in the right places or to sit with arms open, not crossed. People may be very sensitive to strong body language. Keep it in check. Know what you say with your body. Only communicate strong feelings when you feel you have to or when you are certain it will help the situation.

Research shows that in Western cultures, relaxed hands with open palms are often associated with sincerity. Similarly, crossed arms are often associated with defensiveness or aggression. Standing straight and sitting tall signals authority and confidence (moreover, you avoid back injuries). Your tone of voice communicates anger, pleasure, disgust, indifference. Emotional communication plays a large role in the workplace -- too large a role if you are unaware and inaccessible via email.

The safest approach is to mirror the body language of others to make them relax and feel at home. Psychologists note that staying "in sync" with others is a fundamental way to demonstrate that you understand them. You must also respect other people's personal space -- both in terms of distance and what they care about. These vary from person to person, depending on their life experiences, culture, and your relationship with them. There are few general rules. Like animals, we humans defend our territory against others. We claim certain places as our own; we want privileged access to our desk, our bedroom, our house, and our property. We want access to some commodity and to be able to deny or allow access to outsiders at our own liberty. In fact, the British philosopher John Locke (1632-1704) said there were three fundamental longings that were sacred to mankind: life, liberty and property.

You can learn more about yourself and your body language by attending courses in public speaking, exercise, massage, and singing classes to develop the command of your most important communication tool: your voice. Watch yourself on video. Learn by watching yourself practice your speeches and presentations. Allow someone you trust to watch it with you and give you feedback.

Become more aware of your senses[26]

Leaders make better use of their sense perception than others. Are you among them? Following Aristotelian physics, we traditionally speak of five senses – hearing, sight, smell, taste, and touch. There are most certainly others. Gaining currency in the last few years have been cold, heat, pain, body awareness (e.g., direction and depth), and balance. There are more subtle senses, such as hunger, fear, happiness/pleasure, empathy, timing, and intuition – including proximity (i.e., knowing when someone is approaching or being aware of the co-presence of others).[27] The spiritual senses – telepathy, precognition, proximity, and ki – are more contested.

While some work can be done to activate awareness of your own senses, some people have unique capabilities. For instance, it has long been known that bats, dolphins, and even some birds and mammals have the ability to orient themselves through reflected sound. However, humans can as well. When exploring a cave, think of how you will, almost instinctively, say "hooh" -- and then wait for the echo in order to assess the size or shape of the cave and how to proceed. Like avian migratory birds, some humans are also sensitive to magnetic fields, using them for healing abilities or to assist in navigation. Speakers can clap their hands to assess a room's acoustics. Singers do the same to feel the size of the room.

Have you ever felt like someone is watching you, say, during a drive on the highway? Very often, if you turn around, you see that someone in the car next to you was watching you. Why does this happen? Is it random? If not, what governs your sense that you are being watched? The notion that there is a life force, a type of energy that flows all around us and holds it all together, is prevalent in many cultures -- especially Eastern ones. The flow of energy (Ki) is what most aptly explains that experience.

Proximity is the feeling that you are close to somebody, or even the feeling that you are not. People with a good sense of proximity can feel whether other people are around. You may have noticed that people are looking at you and turn toward them. My nine-month-old baby knows when we are home before we enter the house. One might think she hears the elevator -- but she also detects my presence when I enter via the stairs. It is more likely she actually knows.

Proxemics – the study of proximity and body spacing – was coined in 1966 by anthropologist Edward T. Hall. Hall distinguished between intimate, personal, social, and public zones based on distance. Subsequent research has tried to explain how this varies between cultures – Latin cultures and Nordic cultures are thought to be opposites. However, it also depends on the person, gender, situation, and other factors. It is also largely learned, rather than biologically contingent.

The value of sense perception in a given social situation depends on many things: whether you are using them, whether you are willing to put them to use, the context, the time at hand, etc. But just a quick and dirty look at how senses affect leadership is revealing – there is immense untapped potential if you become more aware of touch, proximity, intuition, and ki.

Leadership below the skin – touchy teamwork

Touch is one of the most visible senses in all close relationships. It is evident in affective bonds between family members, friends, enemies, or team mates. A pat on the shoulder as a reward is encouraging to most people. A handshake greets a person in most cultures and seals the deal in many. However, many things are much more subtle than that. Some touching has come to be seen as inappropriate, such as male teachers touching the shoulders of female students. Some cultures are so afraid of public physical contact between people of opposite gender that they prohibit or discourage it.

People traditionally learn through using their hands, handcrafting objects for daily use, decoration, industrial use, and art. More mundanely, we still first experience many things with our hands. We check temperatures, feel ahead of us when walking through a dark room, and investigate objects by feeling around them. In fact, looking at the way we experience the world around us by touch may be an indication that the human mind is not just about the brain. The entire body is a cognitive entity, taking in the world around us.[28] Leaders should take note. The way a culture greets, says goodbye, and expresses gratitude and contempt may well be by touch.

In Japanese Shiatsu massage, which is rapidly gaining currency globally, touching one of the 365 commonly established pressure points affects Ki energy levels in your body, unblocking the energy flow and alleviating pain. If touch can have that effect, soothing words can as well. Very few computers or software programs are able to attune to that.

Despite early experiments, at MIT's The Media Lab, Xerox Corporation's Palo Alto Research Center (PARC), and other places, culturally sensitive, kinesthetic computing is in its infancy.

An initiative that has progressed in this regard, however, is the Sacred World Foundation (SWF)[29] in Dehli, India. It was established by a former PARC engineer and musician, Ranjit Makkuni, who preaches interaction design with Gandhi's principles like truth, non-violence, sensitivity, and self-realization. SWF acts as a museum as well as a breeding ground for 25 future-oriented computer designers using man-made objects from Indian culture interwoven with electronics and digital technology. They build the bridge between technological and traditional cultures in India to redesign technology to meet local user needs, ensure that sacred dimensions are present, and restore the tactile dimension (especially the role of the hand in learning and exploration).

SWF's work incorporates handicraft practices on user interface into digital technologies such as cell phones, computers, and screens, making them more attuned to the Indian experience, culture, and daily life. For example, their Crossing Project[30] seeks to remodel Bamaras (a Ganges River, crossing) using both virtual and spatial means, from the perspective that -- throughout the world, and especially in India -- river crossings are "power spots," or concentrations of nature's energies, a pilgrimage embodying learning and transformation. Letting technology surrender to the human hand, in addition to displays on rectangular screens, SWF uses architectonic space, lightning systems, backdrops, aroma, and wind effects. Lots of high-touch interfaces involve the whole body, simulating the rituals of floating lamps to the river of healing through touch.

Tasteful leadership

Meals pay a huge role in all successful leadership. Beyond being a nutritional necessity, food has a social function. Sharing the experience of food in the moments after it was made -- tasting things, letting others taste, describing food to others while they are there -- is a very powerful thing and leads to bonding and companionship. In the European Commission, inviting colleagues for coffee is a daily ritual. Senior officers always pay. If younger ones offer to pay, there is a moment of confusion. Even at lunch, the hierarchy attempts to assert itself.

Eating a meal together is considered by most cultures as a way of bringing people closer. Exactly how it happens can vary, and care must be taken, especially in today's globalized world. There are vegetarians, allergies, religious prohibitions, personal preferences, and individual moods to be aware of. A good leader understands this and uses his knowledge to bond with colleagues.

In the Norwegian *Julebord* rituals before Christmas, most employers pay for a lavish three- to six-hour meal, followed by a party at which most everyone gets drunk and many embarrass themselves. Like carnival, everyday life and its rules are suspended for one night. Clearly, food is part of any good leadership strategy. In Opentech (see chapter 16), lunch starts at the same time for all employees and the digital bell rings. No meetings are possible – lunch is regarded as together time.

Korean business culture is inextricably linked to the display of social ties through drinking rituals. In fact, drinking is a must. No business takes place before drinking together: Drinking is a social occasion that builds camaraderie. Koreans feel that, since the person will carry out the business, the knowledge, money or resources are only the medium. Thus, camaraderie is the focal point of a business deal. The leader is always in charge, including paying the bill in all social occasions -- whether out drinking the strong Korean liquor Soju, wine, beer; at in a company lunch or dinner; or even paying for women entertainers (the Korean *kisaeng* is a variant of the Japanese geisha). A foreigner would need to pay for all of this in order to do business.

Wine takes on a particular importance in business because it is a symbol of togetherness (friendship, wealth, prosperity) and because it demonstrates sophistication and respect (wine knowledge). The reasons for this are historically complex, but, essentially, wine has distinguished the elite throughout time, because of the possibility to make quality judgments and to display social and economic power -- the availability of inexpensive wine notwithstanding.

Leaders, one could argue, should know wine and have the capacity to deliver meaningful comments about wine. Knowing a bit about the major wine-producing countries (Argentina, Australia, Chile, France, Germany, Italy, South Africa, Spain, and the United States) surely won't hurt. Knowing the distinct tastes of major grape varietals both red wine (Cabernet Sauvignon, Malbec, Merlot, Pinot Noir, Sangiovese, Syrah, Tempranillo, and Zinfandel) and white wine (Chardonnay, Gewürztraminer, Muscat, Pinot Gris, Prosecco, Riesling, and Sauvignon Blanc) is not a bad idea either.

In terms of knowing how to describe wine aromas, an easy reference is the so-called wine aroma wheel developed by Dr. Ann C. Noble, now retired from the University of California - Davis. Here you find a visual overview of most commonly accepted terms for wine, with similar tastes in proximity to one another. The basic aromas are fruity, vegetative, nutty, caramelized, woody, earthy, chemical, pungent, oxidized, microbiological, floral, and spicy. When you talk about wine, you usually distinguish between "on the nose" (smelling it), "on the palate" (tasting it), and "in the aftertaste." White wines can be dry (no residual sugar) or sweet. All wines vary in terms of acidity, bitterness, body, tannins, and alcohol level. As all matters of taste, there should really not be so many rules, since tastes vary. Have words for wine but mean them. Authenticity pays off.

Leadership from below also means to recognize that wine knowledge must be used with care. Never dominate the discussion with mastery of wine terminology -- only use it to enrich people's experience of the wine and the meal and to encourage bonding and conversation over this most delightful symbol of togetherness.

Being heard

Listen up! Hearing is the sense you use when listening to others. Few things are more important than listening. It is a rare skill; it gives you insight in how other people think. Listening is the key to empathy, to hearing the nuances in the speech and voice of others – and to assessing their message based on their presentation.

In technical terms, you may hear people who speak only at certain decibels, generally between 9 and 20000 Hz, though it depends on individuals and situations; you may also sense it directly, as vibrations on your own skin or on objects around you.

Developments in sound technology are astounding. For instance, speakers have now become ultra small, yet capable of high-quality sound. The study of sound – acoustics – is a research area at many universities and quite a few companies. The awareness of quality differences in sound, however, predates the science. One need only think of musical instruments like the ones made by violinmakers Stradivari (1644-1737) and the Guarneri family (operating in the seventeenth and eighteenth centuries).

Leaders should focus on recognizing sound from noise. Nowadays, most humans can only recognize ten birds by name and appearance. Yet they have no problem distinguishing thousands of company brands. Peterson Field Guides[31] must find their equivalent in the management section – knowledge workers want to be heard!

Seeing eye to eye

The most efficient way to convey your point is to meet face to face. But the visual is much more than face-to-face interaction. The visual sense distinguishes between color and brightness. However, a trained eye can also observe depth, perspective, and aesthetic quality.

Social theorist Erving Goffman explored stigma. People have two main reactions: approval or disapproval. The physical signs associated with stigma are constantly evolving. Glasses, for instance, have undergone a re-branding. They are no longer a sign that you have bad eyesight (a stigma). Armani glasses may, in fact, signal to others that you are cool. Having red hair, which used to be a stigma, is similarly popular – to the extent that women actually dye their hair this color by choice as a fashion statement. For me this works out, and somehow takes away the sting off of earlier stigma. The color itself is referred to by many names – red, ginger, orange, copper, or Venetian blond. Positive physical stigma includes attractiveness, a particularly nice smile -- specific attributes that attract attention and exude sexiness.

According to the American socio-biologist Desmond Norris, the way we perceive physical appearance is driven by our biology and our genes. We see fertility as desirable, and fertility is best demonstrated by body type. Body language and kinesthetic research has raised attention to these phenomena for years.

If you want to make a positive impression, a smile is the universal opening statement. Leaders should dress appropriately to context, in sync with others, or consciously deviant. "Take in" people you meet in full and notice if they have a ring on their fourth finger, their watch, their jewelry, their clothes, and shoes – these items can tell you a lot about a person. Read the surroundings with your eyes. Look at the office décor, whether there are family photographs, what books are on the shelves. What is important is to be seen and recognized. To be seen by your boss, but also by your co-workers and your customers. Learning to see what others see is imperative to leaders.

Leadership from below	Lesson #8
Leaders must build awareness of sight, hearing, taste, touch, Ki, intuition, and proximity in order to make full use of sense perception.	

Chapter 9

Leading by intuition

Energy, charisma, and flow – Eastern principles matter in business. But good intuition depends on having a message in the first place. Good leaders, regardless of their origin, combine management with holistic principles.

The energy we send out in all directions, only to be picked up by a few people, constitutes our knowledge flow. These flows originate in individuals, in teams, and even as a result of a strong brand. For example, when an executive overhears your lunch conversation and picks up your idea, passing it off as her own, that's flow. When your colleague forwards your email to someone else who then contacts you -- or puts the knowledge to use even without your knowledge, that's also flow. The effect of branding on your interaction with a company – maybe you buy their products or apply to work there – is yet another example.

While some are more intuitive than others, training yourself can never hurt. Intuition is awareness of the energy flows that surround us. In fact, vital energy, or breath, is called *prana* in the ancient Eastern language Sanskrit, *mana* in Hawaiian, *élan vital* in French, bioenergy in English, "the force" in George Lucas's epic *Star Wars* films, *wakan* in Sioux, *pneuma* in Greek, *chi* in Chinese, and *ki* in Japanese and Korean. The ki concepts point to what makes you energetic, alert, powerfully present. Ki deeply resounds across cultures and is similar to what westerners call intuition.

Intuitively means suddenly, without thought.   Intuition is a domain about which Western science is largely silent. There are few good theories to account for how it works. Some, like the French sociologist Michel Maffesoli and the Norwegian philosopher Arne Næss, claim feelings have a rational base. Feelings, they agree, are formed through some sort of internal decision-making process in our body. French sociologist Pierre Bourdieu calls this process *habitus.*

During my previous work on journal and book publishers (1997), I found that quality judgments of any kind are always based on subjective gut feeling that cannot be explained. One editor said the gut feeling was immediate, upon reading a few pages of text and sometimes in the first paragraph. Aesthetic judgments are often of that kind. However, we can often back them up if we think about them. First impressions are generally quite stable. Famous Austrian art historian Ernst Gombrich (1909-2001) agreed with this: A picture has an immediate effect on the viewer, and this impression seldom changes even if you study the same work of art for years.

Controlling the flow of energy

Eastern medicine, acupressure, Shiatsu massage, and martial arts like Aikido all attempt to manipulate ki. The energy that flows inside you also likely is responsible for interpersonal dynamics – what we more commonly call personal chemistry.

In some scientific experiments, ki is described as a kind of electromagnetic force. The ability to make use of electric impulses – so-called *electroception* – is something we recognize exists in fish, sharks, and rays. Ki is something possessed by every human being to a lesser or greater degree. Learned use of ki makes you a good masseuse, healer, Eastern doctor, or practitioner of martial arts. In Aikido, all emphasis is on using the force of your opponent to your advantage, never adding your own negative force. Jiujitsu, another martial art, preaches the use of both positive and negative force.

An old army intelligence buddy of mine – let's call him Mike – once told me: "You are still a mystery to me. I haven't figured you out yet." I was puzzled at this statement and asked him what he meant. We had known each other for several months, had spent the last month on the same team -- four guys in the same tent, sharing life stories, carrying each other over mountains, withstanding army interrogation training and physical hardship. What could he possibly mean? Mike, who is 6'5", grew up on a farm, was an A+ student in school, excels in all physical army disciplines, and is one of the most intelligent guys I have met. "Well," he said, "I always know what drives a person almost right away, but with you it is different."

I was not fully satisfied with that answer, but I have thought about his approach to other people ever since. I now think I know what he was doing. He was applying his emotional intelligence. Emotional intelligence is the ability to recognize feelings in ourselves and others. Aforementioned psychology writer David Goleman applied emotional intelligence (EQ) to leadership in the 2002 book *Primal Leadership*. Leadership is innate, but many have forgotten how to do it. Both Goleman and my friend Mike have not. Incidentally, I think I also know why I was harder to figure out. I am a sensation seeker, driven by intense emotions wherever they occur. Many knowledge workers are. It has taken psychology some time to come to terms with us. But they are getting there.

"Leadership is innate, but many have forgotten how to do it"

Picking up on your mother's precognition

Whatever you choose to call it -- ki, IQ, or EQ -- some people are able to sense things earlier than others. And I am not talking about an outlandish belief in parapsychology. Your mother knew that something was wrong – even before you told her -- when you came home from school with a bad grade, a black eye, or a guilty conscience. In part, there were subtle signs; in part, she just "knew." How was that possible?

Your mother sensed something with the ki, one might say, or the way her ki met with yours. Being empathetic, she tried to merge with your perspective. She is socially intelligent; she sensed that you approached her differently, noticed that you didn't look straight at her, or took note of how you looked at other people you passed on your way. There could be many explanations. But let us just enter into the logic of ki for a moment. The notion builds on the fact that you as a person constantly interact with others in a physical location. Furthermore, what we traditionally call social interaction consists of a mix of physical, social, and mental processes. These occur in and around your body, and comprise your presence. Becoming aware of ki, you can to some extent control or relay energy to where it is needed the most. However, there is no need to believe in the extreme variants of parapsychology in order to appreciate ki phenomena at their most basic levels. Gestalt psychology, a fairly established brain theory that emerged in the 1930s, holds that the whole is greater than its parts -- directly in line with ki-sensitive thinking.

In the beginning of this book, I described the notion of hyperspacing. Hyperspace is, in fact, a term from quantum physics, which has now largely become mainstream science. In leadership terms, hyperspace is the alignment of all possible impressions, which we utilize with all online and offline resources. We are in a mode that enables us to convince others and engage in placemaking – fixing certain impressions.

In superstring theory, a more controversial area of quantum physics, the hypothesis is that all matter comprises super-thin strings that vibrate, much like a violin, but on infinite frequencies and in multiple spaces. The idea of ki ties in with this, since the electromagnetic energy that surrounds us can sometimes be put to active use when we synchronize breathing or body movements. What actually happens when we produce actionable insight – and earn money doing so – is that we make use of the most basic strings that society and matter are built of.

Martial art – power from below

The best example of ki is found in martial art. Professionals will tell you to take a punch as a challenge, even to appreciate the hit as a gift. A punch allows you to incorporate its devastating power and make use of it, exploiting gravity and momentum. Knowing what to expect from an opponent's force, you can obstruct it or use it yourself, preserving your own mental state untouched by the opponent's energy. Incidentally, if you do not know how dangerous a situation is, you will also perform much better that if you are brought out of balance because you are frightened. I am sure all of you remember anecdotes about individuals who have received remarkable powers for a short instant. You may have had the experience of being able to walk that extra hour even when seemingly super-tired. The reason is that your own ki remains intact; you are fully focused on what needs to be done and not worried about whether it is possible. A similar, but utterly destructive effect can be had from crack cocaine or steroids, but the difference is that naturally induced ki replenishes after you rest.[32] An action carried out with ki appears effortless, even though great energy is exerted.

The ki energy is not abstract when you practice Aikido. In fact, its spatial correlate is *ma*, the appropriate distance between fighters. In martial arts, as well as in a Japanese tea ceremony, there is a structural logic by which the energy plays out even before the physical manifestation. Two masters of martial arts will, in fact, let their energies (ki) fight the battle when standing face to face, almost immobile, sensing each other's powers before the battle. Great generals in history have most certainly had the same experience, sizing up the enemy's forces. Nowadays, in all struggle, the game of hiding your intentions (ki), makes the effort of understanding energy even more important. For instance, it would have been useful if President George W. Bush had accurately assessed Saddam Hussein's power before the second Iraq war. Or, more accurately, the complex power relationships in the region as a whole – where religion, parties and factions matter more than leaders once the strong grip of a dictator is gone.

You need not be a martial arts devotee in order to appreciate this insight; psychologists will tell you the same thing. There is healing power embedded in every tragedy. If a parent dies prematurely, that has an immense impact on your life. Everything stops. You feel empty and devoid of meaning. You want to die. In fact, you even feel dead sometimes. That can last for many months; the loss takes years to soften and will never fully go away. I speak from personal experience.

However, some exceptional individuals are able to draw enormous strength from such an experience, by learning from the incredible zing of emotion and energy the tragedy has caused. If you incorporate the deep awareness that life has a meaning in the moment, you will live more intensely each day and appreciate it.

If you also remember the pain, or know how to express your feelings, you can communicate to others how to deal with sorrow. Only then can you be there for a friend, a colleague, or a stranger who experiences a similar loss. The energy can also be channeled. You have experienced that death is the ultimate finality, something you cannot fight. That can toughen you in all other struggles, especially in the workplace and in your career. It can drive you to do great things, and to accomplish things you never would have, because living now becomes more precious. Whether or not you have had such an experience, learn to recognize the signs around you. Leaders do.

Asian leadership – from mentality to practice

While leading an organization based in another culture is always difficult, leading people in China (if you are a foreigner) is a unique challenge. There is the need to manage and understand change. What happens when cultural homogeneity meets the demands of globalization? Can the expectations of outsiders and markets becoming increasingly important in China be met by the Chinese and vice versa? The Chinese leadership model emphasizes connections, dignity, and trust, which are equally important for

Western leaders. On the other hand, arguably, the Chinese have for some decades been less entrepreneurial. Now that the desire to change is taking hold, this cultural legacy, in turn, provides a challenge in terms of driving results, vision, and customer centricity – with organizational-buy-in from empowered managers.[33]

The head of a major Western professional organization headquartered in Beijing shared the following story with me. She was trying to make the local employees understand that she is only interested in results, not in process. "Please feel free to execute this task in any way you want. Let us talk in a week and see where we are in the process." What followed was something very surprising: "I glanced into a wall of nothingness. There was absolutely no reaction to my proposal."

The Chinese context and their way of doing things do not incorporate improvising, even if they know how to do it. They simply wanted to be told how to do it. Another time she tried the opposite approach: Do this in the following way. One week later, they had completed the task. One month later, she overheard them talking among themselves admitting they had known of a much better way. But saying that to the boss – second-guessing or questioning the boss's judgment -- was out of the question. A third example of the differences between China and the West: My friend must appear at meetings with high-level Chinese government officials or business leaders just to show her Western face, even though her subordinates are the ones doing the project. Apparently, the respect for foreign authorities only works when the "real" foreigner is present in the room. When a local employee represents that same authority, the situation can become embarrassing, and the leader may lose face.

Yan Cheung, chairwoman of paper recycling giant Nine Dragons Paper and one of the wealthiest people in China, is a shrewd saleswoman and dealmaker, and is possibly an exception to the stereotypically Chinese leadership style. Cheung imported advanced machinery and scrap paper from the United States and completely blew away the Chinese competition in that market. She combines Chinese and Western management and culture, but follows the Western principle of punishing and rewarding staff based on performance merit alone. The Chinese would have awarded seniority.[34]

Another unique leader, N.R. Narayana Murthy – founder and chairman of the board of Infosys, the Indian outsourcing company with 80,000 employees -- reportedly practices an his own hybrid leadership – strongly believing in learning from life-and work experience and learning from powerful chance events[35]. With an unpretentious, grounded lifestyle, he is a caring, father-like figure for the employees of Infosys. Among his many sayings:

"I want Infosys to be a place where people of different genders, nationalities, races and religious beliefs work together in an environment of intense competition but utmost harmony, courtesy and dignity to add more and more value to our customers day after day."[36]

With interests that range from computer chips to shipping, Samsung epitomizes South Korea's family-run conglomerates (*chaebol*), which were credited with building the Korean economic miracle from the 1960s to the 1980s. Korean leadership reflects cultural values, such as pride in saving face (*kibun*); allowing personal relations to take precedence over business; and the value of identifying other people's state of mind through understanding non-verbal cues (*nunchi*)[37]. Moreover, Korean society is founded on Confucian principles like harmony (*inhwa*); respect for family, elders, and authority; loyalty, honor, and piety. The heir, Lee Jae

Yong, who is about to take over Samsung, however, takes a more global approach; he is Harvard-educated, with joint degrees from the John F. Kennedy School of Government and the Harvard Business School. Samsung is the trendsetter for corporate Korea. The group accounts for 8 percent of Korea's tax revenues, 22 percent of exports, and almost one-quarter of stock market capitalization.[38] After massive marketing campaigns, Samsung is among the top 100 brands in the world and is about to transcend its origins.

Toyota, the world's largest automaker based on net worth, revenue, and profit squeezes the maximum out of their employees, through their system of continuous improvement (*kaizen*),[39] insisting that knowing by being there (*genchi genbutsu*),[40] digging around for evidence (*namawashi*)[41] always is better; gaining practical experience cannot be substituted by theoretical knowledge. Toyota makes quality everyone's responsibility: Toyota expects people at every level to think and act like quality-control inspectors and to manage individual strengths.[42] Clearly, Toyota in part already practices leadership from below.

Carlos Ghosn, president and CEO of Nissan Motor Co., Ltd. and Renault, turned around Nissan over the past six years similar to the way that Lee Iacocca did with Chrysler: bypassing Japanese management practices and breaking the traditional Japanese business alliances. After touring Nissan plants, he diagnosed the problems and decided the solution was cost-cutting. Refusing to play diplomatically, he dismantled the Fuyo group,[43] the traditional Japanese supplier network (*keiretsu*)[44] on which Nissan had relied; stopped seniority-based promotions. Ghosn concentrated on changing the organizational culture at Nissan. He believes strongly in empowerment, clarity, boldness of vision, hands-on management, work-life balance, and transparency. He briskly closed plants, fired workers, hired stylish new auto designers, and fought with his company's Board of Directors to sell cars with passion -- based on deep knowledge of consumers and his competition. Internally, he established cross-functional teams; copied Renault's career management system; fast-tracked top performers; introduced aggressive performance metrics, linking them to powerful incentives (and punishments); and, thus, broke down silos -- the same way he had done with Renault previously. However, it was all accomplished practically without higher management changes. Ghosn speaks four languages fluently; born in Brazil to Lebanese parents, he grew up and attended Jesuit secondary school in Lebanon; received his higher education in France; and is now French by nationality. Ghosn learned the fine points of marketing and customer satisfaction in the United States and learned business acumen at Michelin and Renault. When hired at Nissan, he immediately started Japanese lessons; he is multicultural, and his global perspective shows.[45] The first foreigner to reach such a senior level in a major Japanese corporation, cleverly exploiting local media to repair Nissan's tarnished image, he has shown that company culture is malleable, and that execution matters more than strategy, but that communication is at the core. Results are the outcome of a credible plan, determination, focus, discipline, and swift execution. Ghosn practices management by example -- an essential component of leadership from below.

The co-founder of Sony Corporation, Akio Morita, had a leadership style that brought about the Sony Walkman; the design and innovation around many new products; brand management strategies; and human resources skills. While committed to creating new lifestyle choices and forms of enjoyment for its customers, Sony still relies on creating a shared social space (ba) among many workers and groups, because each worker has tacit knowledge that can only be mobilized in those settings, according to Nonaka (1996), the Japanese management scholar. Nonaka goes far in suggesting that management and training don't transmit knowledge as efficiently as through *ba* relationships. Nobuyuki Idei, Morita's successor, saw significant losses; the current CEO, Howard Stinger, is also in a bit of trouble with the insiders by refusing to move to, or establish residence in Tokyo; in fact, he lives in a hotel. Managers still handle problems in the traditional Sony way: quietly and without informing top executives.[46] At present, Sony, it seems, is in full tension between the traditional Japanese ways and the more global trends that threaten to undermine its culture, but also seem needed in order to excel in a competitive space. Leadership from below, which takes its point of departure from the local surroundings, must here be reconciled with the new, more open spatial orientation which follows from a global market, consumers and workforce.

To further clarify the Eastern influence, we will now discuss charisma, a global phenomenon that is effective due to the principles already discussed (mainly ki) but that also has had a Western cultural wrapping for some time.

Charisma - leadership from within

The German sociologist Max Weber (1864-1920) introduced the concept of charisma to account for the process by which radical change is brought about in societies and organizations.[47] He found there were three legitimate sources of authority throughout history: traditional, bureaucratic-legal, and charismatic authority.

What is charisma? It is tempting to think that typical CV qualities, such as experience, education, and skills, would enhance charisma. One could also think that the attributes we display or convey at meetings and interviews will count, such as physical appearance, charm, and social background. However, it may be that we have to dig deeper into the psychological repertoire of a charismatic person, and what has shaped his or her development, to find the source of others' fascination. What is the source of charismatic energy? Can you develop your charisma to be a better leader?

The short answer is that you can use leadership from below to build charisma and to develop a powerful presence if you are motivated to make a difference in every encounter. It is the road to moral, visionary leadership with greater goals in mind.[48]

"People are interested in the person who is interested in them"
– Dale Carnegie

Finding your own charisma

To build charisma, you must be passionate. Challenge people around you to act. Commit to a worthy cause. Make sacrifices. Inspire others. Build a circle of followers. Preach your message regularly. Keep it simple. Adjust when circumstances change. Charisma builds naturally to some degree in any successful team process, regardless of what charismatic qualities you believe you possess. However, a leader initially driven by charisma usually does not prevail. In fact, charisma is something which is built between people under extreme conditions, not something individuals possess regardless of circumstance. Charisma takes quite an effort to sustain.

You can indeed develop charismatic behavior even if you are not often thought of as a leader. Try to remember a time when you were the de facto leader, the emerging leader, or just were able to make a difference because of a specific situation. Charismatic leaders in one context may not be recognized as such by the larger community. Regardless, it is essential to learn how to spot charisma in action. Charisma, when effectively deployed, is a resource. Learn to recognize it in others and in yourself.

Knowledge workers typically experience charisma at work when listening to the best C-level executives or keynote speakers at conferences. However, you may have encounters that bring out charismatic qualities in a one-on-one situation as well.

Can the Internet transmit charisma? How does charisma come into play in a virtual work team? The charismatic tool par excellence -- the inspirational speech -- is less compelling when delivered by email or transmitted via video-link. When I worked for the European Commission, I rarely watched a full video of our top leader, although I seldom left the room when she was speaking live. Online, restraints are absent. You are free to leave. The only exception is if you have paid $30 for a half-hour Internet access at a hotel.

Also absent are the compelling aspects of presence: physical cues, as well as the audience's reactions. Online tools have failed to replicate the effect that observers have on the way we communicate. If you ever have participated in a phone or videoconference, you know the feeling.

The MIT Media Lab is currently experimenting with a cell phone that provides location-specific mood and compatibility signals. We are constantly trying to create technology that mirrors life. There is a long way to go.

Create team spirit

Team spirit is called for when we rally around high school sports. What exactly do we mean when we say team spirit in a business context? One way to see it: creating a sense of common purpose, a shared sense of urgency and identity with task, team, and outcome. Psychologically, what happens? Should team spirit still matter?

Opinions differ. Some argue that we are moving into an era in which online relationships perfectly mirror offline ones; they claim that the Internet makes us borderless, heralding the "death of distance."

On the other hand, literature from fields such as psychology, sociology, and management indicates that handshakes count more than documents, phone conversations, or emails with the same message. This is particularly true in conflicts or early-phase meetings. Why is proximity more important at the beginning of virtual teamwork? How often do we need face-to-face interaction? Obviously, it depends on a variety of factors, but, yes, all teams should meet early and as often as possible.

Leadership from below	Lesson # 9
Successful leaders combine Eastern life principles and Western management principles. Charismatic leaders have a strong presence, are aware of how energy flows through human encounters. Energy (ki) is they key to health, intuition, as well as innovation.	

Chapter 10

Controlling your environment

Physical objects are of crucial importance to any knowledge environment. Do not merely accept the surroundings as given. Take charge of all your resources.

French sociologist Bruno Latour[49] has written about our power to enlist nature as our ally. The microbe, for instance, was a non-human object with properties unknown to man before another Frenchman, the doctor Louis Pasteur, started to speak on its behalf. Pasteur claimed that microbes contribute to disease and contamination. So, says Latour, it was Pasteur who gave microbes power.

With Latour's example in mind, try to conjure a picture in your mind about nature – trees, flowers, paths, mountains, rivers, etc. – and ponder if it impacts your work. Nature can help us relax, if we make use of it. But as flexible as nature is, it is constrained by its own properties: A small lake will remain a small lake, regardless the size of your boat – it will only *feel* smaller. Likewise, designed objects – often called artifacts – are constrained by the people who made them. The designer's ideas, designs, and final product can only do what they intended. Right?

Wrong! Leaders control objects, navigating consciously between them. Handling a computer search, for instance, requires skills. If you are an executive with access to multiple office locations, choosing in which physical location to spend your day is a strategic choice. Depending on the situation at hand, what you achieve -- and, in the end, your routines -- it is an art in itself.

When I was writing my PhD, I sometimes would go directly to my favorite coffee shop in the morning and remain there for a good part of the day, taking notes, thinking, gaining some breathing space from the office, the library, the computer, or my supervisor, for that matter. Not because I planned to do so but because I suddenly got an idea and was immersed in flow – in "the zone" -- for hours at a time. Sometimes you don't want to interact with other people; you just want to watch and observe them – or blissfully ignore them – which requires you to be in the presence of people to ignore.

Every day, just walking around, you choose objects on which to focus your attention and which to ignore. You also deal with the consequences of those choices. For example, you may decide to spend your salary on baby clothes, wine, or dentist bills. Both in your social and professional lives, you have many times throughout the day to decide where to spend your time, whom to talk to, and whom to call. Likewise, you should be equally conscientious about your choice of online resources. Should you invest in a new laptop,

PDA, training, computer infrastructure? Or in programs that would make your career more efficient? But you also have to know how these objects affect your work, and you should monitor their effect on others. An object's power does not reside in the object itself but, rather, in how we use it. By employing knowledge technologies, you delegate tasks to machines. This can be smart, but a PDA can waste your time, and email can bog you down.

If you are trying to start a company, there are many open issues. Every day is up for grabs, so to speak. There are no rules. Nobody tells you what to do; nobody helps you to distinguish what is important and what is not. Whom should you see today? What things should you buy to start up? What documents should you produce? Should you work on the business plan or conduct more research on a competing product? To avoid wasting time, we must make wise choices.

Knowing when, how, and what to delegate is the essence of leadership from below. Remember, by letting others set up your computer, decide what software should be available, what programs to use, what your office should look like, where each team member's office will be located, you let others affect your immediate environment. Co-workers whose desks face each other collaborate much more than those who do not. People on the same floor are more prone to work together as well – or go to lunch together.

Feng shui, the ancient Chinese practice of placement and arrangement of space to achieve harmony with the environment, implies that office clutter, windowless offices, and lack of personal space (so one can establish territory) can slow down the flow of energy (ki). Business trips must also be arranged so that the hotel room bed is supported by a wall, that you bring personal items to make the room your own (a picture of your family, a scent, or water spray), immediately open a window to let in fresh air (your air), and close to a favorite restaurant -- otherwise business trips will drain too much energy and will be counterproductive.[50]

If you do not care at all about location, you are not a leader in your own life. Deciding *where* you should spend your energy will put you in charge of your own environment. You will lead the objects and not be led by them.

Attach yourself to people and things

Psychological research is particularly useful for leadership from below, because psychology goes to the core of relationships – what leadership is about. In his groundbreaking lecture "The Making and Breaking of Affectional bonds," British psychologist John Bowlby[51] posited that early family relations generally give children a "secure base." All future relationships, even in adulthood, are modeled on these childhood relationships. Having a sound "attachment profile" with healthy relationships to significant others also shapes all subsequent learning and development. Bowlby then surveyed what happens when, at an early age, we lose touch with those we love. He observes that if one has never had a positive "model relationship to turn to,", any crisis will inevitably become more serious, and any difficulty with learning will become more serious. Learning is attachment, and you can only attach to what you know.

The workplace is a breeding ground for attachment. Leaders identify with work and the people with whom they work. Building lasting relationships that go beyond the organization or task is important for personal and professional growth. In fact, as a successful knowledge worker, you are likely to identify strongly with one or several communities of practice.

Objects also breed attachment. The process starts early in life. If you are not familiar with computers from early age, you will not feel like you master them. Today's five- to fifteen-year-olds grew up with fairly advanced computer games. Their visual acuity has developed accordingly. Their ability to recognize moving objects is very high. This helps them in many tasks that are crucial to knowledge work.

When I say "attach," I actually mean *attach*. Social engagement with objects is possible. Objects become a key part of our reality. Multimedia permeates our daily lives and fills our homes. We even take it to bed. Each new product design brings changes to how we work and spend our spare time – some superficial, some more profound changes. The question in 2007-2010 is whether purely human environments are becoming old legacy environments and not the dominating ones. In many ways, the new primordial connectedness is with markets, screens, computers, code, and information. People interact so directly with technological objects that many of us are part-man, part-tech – in other words, we become cyborgs, bionic humans. Spending more than 15 hours a day in front of a computer screen may also qualify to cyborg status. The primary relationship for many knowledge workers is with the screen -- not with their cat, dog, or significant other. Some may see this development as scandalous; to others, it is liberating.

To put it in metaphorical terms: A screen is a building site upon which we build our own identity. For instance, one could envisage a government website offering secure, personalized access to all information the government has collected about each citizen. The site does not itself maintain the information but, rather, builds it on your request; the site does not store the information but merely collects it from elsewhere, displaying "you" when you call upon it. It becomes the official, online version of you -- or, at least, the governmentally relevant aspects of you. For example, the Norwegian government currently offers each citizen access to information about him/her contained in population registries, marital status, , and entitlements – but not all in one place. Soon, as it becomes more complete, it will contain most of the officially relevant aspects of your digital identity. The government has dubbed the project "My Page" – soon it will be "the page that *is* me," which is different. This brings us back to the issue of attachment. Loss of data will have consequences in your real life; you may be erased. Entitlements to social benefits will disappear. If there is backup, or a manual procedure, you may be able to restore it. Regardless, make sure you attach yourself to the right people and to the right things. You never know when you will need them the most.

Legacy environments – what we must take as given

Legacy environments are the physical infrastructure and objects that remain important and cannot be wished away, such as large computer systems purchased long ago. However, daily work-life requires ancient technologies such as pens, pencils, and paper and also century-old technologies like desks, telephones, whiteboards, and copy machines, which also become legacy, because they remain your tools. These days, work occurs in designed spaces such as meeting rooms, offices, libraries, work spaces, canteens – and occasionally in restrooms. Newer technologies like screens, displays, email, Internet, personal digital assistants (PDAs), and mobile phones are rapidly moving into the workplace – maybe for good. The importance of work in transient spaces such as airports, elevators, escalators, and sidewalks – which French anthropologist Marc Auge calls "non-spaces," for their lack of unique characteristics – is increasing. Contemporary city dwellers arguably spend less and less time in[52] public spaces like parks, piazzas, and markets, which then gets compensated online – since both business and life itself is built on encounters.

The challenge of juggling all these items is especially large when working with large, established organizations. Too many resources at hand can be overwhelming. Knowledge workers in start-ups have the opposite problem: They struggle to provide enough and adequate resources fast enough to maintain the innovative process.

Among all the objects that occupy a leader's daily life, the Post-it note deserves particular mention, to which we will now turn for a moment.

Preserving personal knowledge with the sticky note

All places on the globe to which the American multinational company 3M has reached through marketing have desks and office cabinets filled with yellow, green, pink, and lavender adhesive paper quadrilaterals. The main use of sticky notes is to adhere small messages to paper, books, and other flat surfaces, directing attention, setting priorities, and jogging memories. Sticky notes allow you to structure documents according to your own head and to add your own personal touch with jotted comments. This allows you to quickly go back and find what was most relevant to you.

In 1968, 3M researcher Spencer Silver tried to make a strong adhesive. He failed; gave up the dream; and shelved his adhesive prototype for a new type of glue. In 1974, a colleague, Art Fry, used the glue on a piece of paper as a bookmark in his choir hymnal. After a while, even 3M discovered that Silver's failed attempt had a much more creative usage, but it was another six years before the product itself was put on the global market. So, you can say, we have today's sticky note because of a combination of Silver's failure and Fry's frustration.[53] Necessity is the mother of invention.

Obviously, there are many other uses. Creative methods that expand the use of sticky notes beyond simply putting them on your desk include: (a) getting information into chunks; (b) organizing papers; (c) brainstorming; (d) mapping relationships; or (e) visualizing an existing process.[54] The European Commission's Joint Research Centre (JRC) of in Seville, Spain, uses sticky notes for brainstorming with experts.

From paper to paperless and beyond

Papyrus, an old form of paper, was used already in Mesopotamia in the ancient Middle East. Paper has been our preferred medium for storing, displaying, and remembering information, culture and knowledge for centuries.

In the last decade, the vision of a paperless existence has started to gain ground. The paperless office was an idea some companies have tried to put to use. In 2002, the Scandinavian telecommunications company Telenor moved to their new headquarters. "Six-thousand employees now have the opportunity to work practically anywhere, anytime," said CEO Jon Fredrik Baksaas.[55] Offices are organized into working units of 30 people, in a configuration that maximizes natural lighting and offers views of the Oslo fjord. This sounds great on paper.

To their dismay, the style did not fit all of their knowledge workers, especially older workers who were used to having their own office. Some younger employees to whom I spoke were also not fully convinced. For instance, there far too little space allowed for personal items and archives. The facility was fully functional in 2007 – but also full of paper.

In 2000, the Estonian government went paperless. Prime Minister Mart Laar was behind the move: "We had no information flow, so moving to a digital information flow was not so hard." His point is that legacy environments, older technologies or processes we cannot just get rid of bring challenges in making new and old technologies talk to each other. Every government and consultant working for them has had that experience.

Leaders understand that the efficiency gains do not necessarily lie in removing all paper flow immediately but, rather, in gradually implementing new routines and making wise judgment calls. They establish fruitful archiving routines, try to read and store most documents on a screen, and do not panic if they see a book of a pile of documents somewhere. The paperless office may never appear. There are even people who point to the soothing smell of paper as one reason they refuse to move on.

There are exceptions to this rule. In 2005, the Danish government implemented e-invoicing by simply shutting off the paper channel. The mission was successful[56], despite some initial difficulty.[57]

"The paperless office may never appear"

Is the office still relevant?

Most of us take for granted that we have office space. But if you have worked for a start-up, you know what it is to manage without one. It is not that glamorous. Knowledge workers need stability and space to think; without that, all of the moving about is in vain. You need to have a product; you need to focus; and you need access to your team members in a private setting conducive to productivity. When I created a company many years ago, the very fact of not having an office while running around trying to sell my business plan became a problem. We met at coffee shops, at home, and discussed in the car, even in the street – but it got tiring. Customers may not have noticed. When we finally moved into an office, in a fabulous dockside development, we quickly and with pride acquired a sense of place. We always met people at their offices, not ours. Will the office die? It is unlikely.

Leadership from below	Lesson # 10
Identify empowering objects and put them to work for you. Decide where you need to be, and spend time in the locations that matter the most to you. Make objects your own.	

Chapter 11

Dealing with Diversity

Culture matters if people bring it up. If they do, you cannot ignore it. Explore differences where they show up. Test stereotypes; do not just accept them as given. Be clear in your demands, and ensure that you are understood. Come to terms with the differences that make a difference.

While difference is the source of innovation, it is also the source of frustration. Some important variables of relevance to leadership from below are age, gender, personality, intelligence, status, experience, mother tongue, language barriers, skills in operating language, pidgin skills (mediating language), team skills, culture, generation, and also time and task motivation. The degree to which people are willing to invest in the team experience matters as well. Just ask them.

Geert Hofstede's[58] 1980 book, *Culture's Consequences*, became an instant success. The Dutch management scholar, today arguably Europe's most influential management thinker, studied IBM employees in 50 countries and found that they differed along several dimensions: power distance (the degree to which there are gaps in power and influence between employees, managers, and executives); individualism (whether the individual counts more than the group or collective); aggressiveness (masculinity v. femininity); uncertainty avoidance (comfort with ambiguity); and long-term orientation (short- or long-term time horizon).

In Hofstede's study, communist countries China and Russia scored high on power distance, while stable democracies like The Netherlands, the United States, and Germany scored low. The United States scored high on individualism, while Indonesia and China scored low. Hierarchical, relatively homogeneous states like France, Japan, and Russia scored high on uncertainty avoidance, while cultural melting pot Hong Kong scored low. China scored high on long-term horizon; Russia and Western Africa scored low.

Anyone who has worked with people from different cultures knows the story is much more complex. What if you have a Danish boss who is a devout Catholic? She may be more hierarchically minded than her more secular Danish peers. Clearly there are many intervening factor that could explain how your boss behaves. You will have to judge what traits come to the surface and which, in the end, make a difference. Hofstede's data is by any measure outdated: His original fieldwork was carried out in 1974, and some of these dimensions are sensitive to historical changes. His data has other limitations – it is a national sample not taking into account regional differences. There are many more dimensions of culture.

In his 1997 book, *Cultures and Organizations, Software of the Mind: Intercultural Cooperation and its Importance for Survival*, Hofstede says culture manifests itself as a set of mental programs -- knowledge structures that influence memory and forgetting. The book ventures into organizational culture as well. Hofstede makes sweeping generalizations, and his categories have a Western bias. It is true that phenomena like culture shock, ethnocentrism, stereotyping, and differences in language and in humor follow certain patterns. However, the flows of globalization intensify cultural interaction. Knowledge workers in multinational companies move around. The more recent World Values surveys[59], led by University of Michigan political scientist Ronald F. Inglehart, are representative national surveys of the basic values and beliefs of publics in more than 65 societies on all six inhabited continents, containing almost 80 percent of the world's population. Evidently, values are a complex matter. Nevertheless, Hofstede brings home the point well: Culture matters in business.

Cross-cultural intelligence is the awareness of ethnic, professional, and company cultures that matter in today's workplace. In fact, possible sources of diversity include race, sex, religion, age, ethnicity (country of origin), gender, sexual orientation (bisexual, heterosexual, homosexual, transgender), marital status, family status, personality traits, area of specialization, technology interest, clothing style, and appearance. These may not turn out to matter at all, unless these differences become a topic. Some traits go deeper than others. I have found that gender, ethnicity, and religion always are issues to be sensitive about.

The chance of potential culture clashes in American workplaces might increase with the influx of highly skilled foreign workers, mainly in the technology field, entering the United States on H-1B work visas. According to figures released by the U.S. Citizenship and Immigration Services, hundreds of thousands of H-1B visas are granted every year. The presence of international workers in the United States is growing rapidly. The same trend occurs in Europe and in Asia.

Strategies to deal with diversity in the workplace are clear. Multidisciplinary leadership and multicultural awareness training become essential. But exactly how that is to happen is more complex, and the team setting is a good example.

Global teams: culture at play

Global teams have the challenge of physical distance, multiple time zones that constrain meeting times, and cultural differences. It is one thing to manage a team. It is another thing to manage a global team. Luckily, they rarely exist. That is, you may have team members who represent different cultures, but you will never have all the tribes of the world represented in one.

The potential diversity of the world is stunning, both in number and qualitative differences. While there are currently 192 member states of the United Nations (2008), the CIA Factbook 2007 has 265 entities (nations, dependent areas or other entities). In addition, ethnicity, culture, race, religion, and language have divided states into separate political, cultural, and linguistic entities as much as history, physical terrain, political fiat, or conquest. There are at least 6,912 known living languages, according to Ethnologue.com, an encyclopedic reference work.[60] Since there are individuals who have mother tongues you would never understand, you have little access to their home ground. That may or may not matter for your leadership, depending what you are trying to accomplish.

A more realistic situation, faced by increasing numbers of managers as well as team members, is to be a member of a team with evident cultural differences. You may very probably in your work-life be confronted with creating, leading, or taking part in a multi-sector, multi-cultural, or multi-national team. To some, this is your everyday reality.

The impact of differences is always difficult to assess. The visible differences in skin tone, working language ability, work styles, and relations with authority may be apparent but may not produce a problem. Sometimes the hidden and subtle differences like unique personal experiences, personality, and motivation produce more pressing issues. Regardless, the problems amplify when using online technologies, since you cannot always see the effect of the message you try to communicate.

The most important thing to establish right away is some common ground. Whether this is based on a common understanding of the importance of the task at hand or a common interest in Japanese manga is less important. What you need to figure out is if there are commonalities or where to go to flush them out. Without that, the team will collapse right from the start.

The process can take anywhere from five minutes to a lifetime, depending on your ambition. There are many facets. Sometimes this can be frustrating. However, bonding in the workplace can create powerful spillover knowledge and a few deeper work relationships can provide both comfort and assistance far beyond the current task you have before you. Moreover, it is fun to form friendships with a diverse range of coworkers and allows you to live your life while working.

If you want to understand thinking style, learn their language (or at least develop an appreciation for the way it sounds, know something about it, and express your desire to learn more). If you want to understand day-to-day life, learn about their food, find restaurants that serve it, cook it yourself, and have them bring in their favorite food so the team can share the joys. If you want to understand their culture, learn about their literature, and read their most important three to ten books (or, at least, excerpts).

If you want to understand their emotional landscape, listen to their music; if you play an instrument, you may wish to play it yourself or bring CDs or music files into team sessions. If you want to understand their personality, ask them about their childhood and upbringing, how their national identity plays out, and about their ambitions – why are they here, in this job?

Most teams have a lot in common by virtue of being called together. They may soon agree on a working language – often English – that puts some cultures in the leading seat already. But on the other hand, the mother tongue issue may not dominate if there are strong pidgin versions spoken in the group.

Some key questions to ask in this situation:

- How do you portray your own heritage, values, and beliefs to your staff and co-workers? How do you respond to theirs?

- How comfortable are you working with people who speak, act, or think differently?

- Do you have a culturally sensitive work or management style? If not, determine exactly what that would entail.

- Do you expect your own practices to set a standard for how other team members work and behave together, or do you think this is negotiated between yourselves?

Thinking through your own experience will position you favorably for the cultural challenge.

The Scandinavian worker's collective

Norway, a small Scandinavian kingdom at the northern tip of Europe, is one of the richest countries in the world. It is the largest oil and gas exporter per capita, and almost all of the wealth creation is funneled back to the citizenry. At $260 billion, the Norwegian Pension Fund, comprising state earnings from oil exploration, is one of the biggest funds on NASDAQ and Dow Jones [61]. The fund's ethics committee recently made it de-invest in The Boeing Company and Lockheed Martin Corporation because of their role in the weapons industry and particularly for taking part in the development of long-range atomic missiles. Norway has twice declined membership in the European Union by referendum (1972 and 1994) and is fiercely independent.[62]

The economy prospers, and the United Nations ranks Norway as one of the top places to live in the world. To some, the cold climate is a deterrent, but that is really another story. Norwegian companies like Statoil and Hydro are at the forefront of the oil industry, and companies like FAST (bought by Microsoft in 2008), and Opera are at the forefront of the IT industry. For example, the Norwegian stock market was up 60 percent in 2005, when its U.S. and European counterparts were either flat or in single-digit growth.

Scandinavian countries combine welfare with growth. Having successfully applied painful reforms during the oil crisis of the 1970s, they transformed themselves into open societies, well prepared for globalization.[63] While industry can hire and fire much more freely than in the rest of Europe, huge welfare benefits provide a safety net for those citizens between jobs.

Scandinavian countries are well known for an egalitarian culture with low power distance; a large, efficient public sector; and low tolerance for elitism. Further, Scandinavia boasts a highly educated and relatively homogeneous workforce; strong unions; centralized negotiation systems; large social democratic parties with strong links to national trade union federations; parties that, for long periods of time, have led governments; and relations between trade unions and employers that are, to a large extent, regulated by laws and central agreements. Democracy in the workplace has also increased knowledge worker productivity.

Norway has publicly endorsed Leadership from below principles for thirty years. In Norway in the 1970s, employees obtained the right to elect one-third of the members of the company's general's assembly, a body composed of all shareholders that meets once a year. The Norwegian Work Environment Act of 1977 gave workers extensive rights to stop production that was dangerous to their health. New procedures were established that gave workers a say in their own work environment issues, and employers who did not fulfill the new work environment requirements were sanctioned.

Much of this legislative work was the result of research on industrial democracy and its effect on productivity and worker welfare. Norwegian researchers discovered that self-managed working groups performed better than traditional hierarchical work. Moreover, in the 1960s, union representatives, workers, and industry association representatives negotiated around the same table for the first time. Another notion also emerged -- action research, a type of consulting in near dialogue between industry and academia – way before this became common elsewhere. This very early experience was to shape the contemporary debate about teams in the workplace.

In Scandinavia, trade unions have served as the vehicles for industrial democracy by advancing the interest of the workers' collective. The workers' collective is a concept developed by the

Norwegian sociologist Sverre Lysgaard who discovered the informal norms shared by all workers. In particular, the worker's collective had strict but unwritten codes for how workers should behave in relation to management and the rationality of technical-economic organization. You should, for instance, never work so fast that you broke the "accord," the established average productivity rate that all workers were able to perform well.

According to Lysgaard, the strength in the workers' collective comes from the 'we' feeling created by shared experiences. The basis for this we feeling is physical proximity at the workplace, which makes interaction possible. Similar working conditions, he argued, makes workers identify with each other and interpret problems in a similar way. The norms of the workers' collective define what it means to be a good workmate as well as what it means to be a traitor. The workers' collective is a buffer between the individual worker and management's interests in shaping the technical-economic organization of the workplace. The Norwegian experience is leadership from below -- a collective effort based on solidarity, shared values, and proximity.

In 2004, Norway mandated 40 percent female representation on company boards; in 2006, they beguan enforcing this rule with financial consequences. Gender equality programs guarantee nine months of government-paid parental leave from work after the birth of a child -- six months of which may be paternity leave.

The Scandinavian incentive system permeates the entire society, creating a minimum of trust and a social capital network partly guaranteed by the state, partly encouraged and flowing from it. The welfare-model thinking even exists in criminal environments. It is reported widely that the Norwegian underworld pays "social security" contributions to families with one member in jail. How the system works is not entirely clear. A similar structure actually exists among extremists in the Middle East, where it is now commonly known that the family of Palestinian suicide bombers has received compensation.[64]

Egalitarian leadership

The best aspect of hierarchy is the rewarding of skill, quality, and excellence. Hierarchy values leadership, purpose, direction, vision, and efficiency. Egalitarian leadership, on the other hand, is based on democratic values, inclusiveness, relationships, listening, and compassion.

Open Source logic (discussed in chapter 16) is based on the ability to influence through exchange of gifts, as well as being drawing consensus and awarding excellence based on the assumption that the best always floats to the top. For this to happen, evidently, there is a non-hierarchical requirement, a strong respect for others and rapid change of leadership. All groups must have potential access to leadership.

Other examples of egalitarian ways are: teams in general, the terror network Al Qaeda, special forces teams, the ideal democracy, some tribes (for example, the Quapaws, a Native American tribe from Arkansas, was egalitarian[65]), as well as many Scandinavian companies.

Strikingly enough, the terror network Al Qaeda[66] has proved to be both efficient and capable of withstanding fierce opponents like Western military and intelligence, the isolation of their leadership, and the geographical spread of their activities. Al Qaeda started with charismatic founders like Osama Bin Laden who hijacked a powerful ideology from fundamentalist factions of Islam. Combined with the evolving idea of network organizing, and their ingenious and disastrous planning culminating in high-visibility terrorist attacks, the momentum of the events of September 11 inspired a seemingly ever-growing number of cells that work almost independently, with very little need for central coordination, and with extreme devotion and loyalty to the task. The organization is the dream of any executive. Few have figured out exactly how it all works, and many of the members do not even know or care. Leadership without a leader sounds strange. But leadership codes are often embedded in the community, in the fabric of society itself.

Scandinavian leaders

Scandinavian companies like Telenor, Volvo, and IKEA practice egalitarian leadership. The human factor is high on the priority list. Leaders often seek validation and input from employees on key decisions, and there is a regulatory system in place that protects employees. On the other hand, with increasing international influence, foreign employees sometimes have to "play Swedish" in order to fit in[67]. What also tends to happen is that subsidiaries develop separate company cultures that become a hybrid form – egalitarian but adapted to the local needs.

The Danish-born president of IKEA North America, Pernille Spiers-Lopez, embodies the Scandinavian leadership model – a woman and a mother with teenage kids:

I am very aware of the necessary give-and-take between the importance of my work and of my life at home. My husband and I respect each other's time and needs, and that solid foundation of an extremely supportive family allows me to feel good about what I do at work. You also need an understanding culture in the workplace or it will be a tough struggle.[68]

In fall 2003, *Working Mother* magazine named IKEA North America one of the 100 best companies for working mothers.[69] IKEA, privately held since its founding in 1943, is based in Sweden and has 90,000 employees in its 227 stores in 33 countries, with operations in 44 countries, and global sales at nearly $20 billion. It specializes in fashionable furniture and home accessories at low prices, scouting out new designers who work for less. The IKEA way combines a very Scandinavian embrace of employment policies, a social safety net, and a strong drive for profits and market share.

IKEA practices a form of "gentle coercion" to keep a customer in the store as long as possible. At the entrance, you can drop off your kids at the playroom, an amenity that encourages more leisurely shopping. When tired after walking around the large facility, the famous Swedish meatballs are served in the luxurious cafeteria; the cafeteria is positioned at the strategic point before you descending the stairs half-way into the store, thereby luring families into another two hours of shopping.

The IKEA catalogue is the company's most important marketing channel. Last year, a total of 160 million copies were printed in 52 editions and 25 languages. In Scandinavia, no home is complete without it, and it can be the subject of small talk and intense discussion into the late hours, even at student parties. The IKEA catalogue is a cult object of the young and trendy, because the designs are cool and affordable to students as well as young families; because "everyone" has a piece of their catalogue in their living room; because it defies elitism (and therefore is loathed by some); and because if you have experienced the self-assembly furniture, you can share the experience of sweating over your new purchase. Their instructions are famously unintelligible, and everybody has at some point discovered product parts are missing or damaged.

"You can take IKEA out of Småland, but you can't take Småland out of IKEA," the company says on their own website. "Småland, where the company's founder was born and raised, can be easily identified

as the source of our shared values. Simplicity, humility, thrift and responsibility are all evident in the lifestyle, attitudes and customs of the place where IKEA began. An example of the Smålanders' way of doing things is not to ask others what you should be doing, but to ask yourself and then get on with it!"

Egalitarian leadership can also pose challenges. McKinsey & Company worked for a Scandinavian natural resources conglomerate that was struggling to compete in the global market and wanted to determine if its managers could handle future challenges. The client leadership team was eager to provide development opportunities for managers, but, because of the company's egalitarian culture, it had never openly discussed promotions, leadership selection, or management development. By positioning the initiative as "leadership development," McKinsey was able to help the Scandinavian company make leadership a priority.[70]

The Scandinavian, or Nordic, model of a strong welfare state and stakeholder capitalism is traditionally stronger than the more traditional business ideology of "shareholder value." In Scandinavia, the rise of the upper middle class in the private sector is felt as a threat against the traditional regime, since it leads to increasing income gaps and to a decline in status for the historically more powerful political and organizational elites.[71] The economies of the Nordic societies are small and open, and one could wonder whether the same principles would work elsewhere. The European Union, for one, is now looking to Scandinavia to fix its economic growth; yet the EU seeks to maintain the social models in the 25 member states.

There are hardly generic leadership traits between cultures, some will say. However, to the extent you believe in cultural differences at all, it also applies to leaders, even if they are internationally minded. For example, in the Asian, Scandinavian, and, Dutch cultures, the excessive expression of individuality is considered socially undesirable. In these cultures, singling out individuals with public praise is likely to result in embarrassment, rather than gratification.

Egalitarian culture fosters a set of common beliefs giving value to positive communication, the cooperative workplace, active information flow, and employee empowerment. Egalitarian leadership is ideologically placed in a democratic system with some degree of shared vision of what society should be, relatively open communication, a large degree of confidence and trust in subordinates, and in the notion that subordinates' ideas should be put to use.

When ethnicity comes to the surface

Obviously, complexity increases when more variables are present. However, the mere existence of differences does not necessarily mean those differences will come to the surface. Or, that they should be mentioned. One example: Bill is a successful businessman, a C-level executive. Because of a corporate takeover, he suddenly has to work closely with Joe, who is in similar position in the firm that was taken over. On his first day at Bill's office, Joe mentions that he knows they will work closely together and says, "The fact that you are black does not matter to me." Bill is shocked since it is has been ten years since he even thought about his ethnic background in a work context. It was always taken for granted that he was a successful person based on merit alone. Although Joe meant no harm (in fact, Joe is especially sensitive to race, as he is married to an American Indian and has a half brother who is Jewish), the teamwork between Bill and Joe is off to a bad start. The lesson: Where race, religion, sexual orientation, political affiliation, health status, or any number of sensitive identity matters are concerned, figure out whether an issue is really an issue *before* you mention it. Sensitive issues are always sensitive. And first impression matters.

Diversity between industry sectors

Knowledge workers today must operate across sectors. That can be challenging. Naturally, a team in the health sector faces different challenges than a team in the automotive industry, both in the nature of their work and in the requirements (legal, social, economic) and resources available. In fact, sector variables may produce radically different tasks, motivations, challenges, and opportunities. When you have to work together, assumptions (those things taken for granted) may be wrong. Tread carefully. Ask twice; experiment -- especially if you work with sectors that are unfamiliar to you.

Usually, there are collaboration issues between government, business, and nonprofit organizations. If laypeople are involved, as representatives of customers or citizens, they will not know the context in which their input will be used. Stakeholder requirements differ between and even within sectors such as high-tech, manufacturing, and services. There are regional differences, as well.

Kjell Inge Røkke, a Norwegian businessman, is both atypical and extremely successful. A dyslexic fisherman, told by a schoolteacher that he'd never amount to anything, at age 18, Røkke went to Seattle, where he sold fish off a boat. There he launched the enterprise that would bring his fortune: buying up boat after boat, all old honks; ruthlessly and fiercely pushing his crews to the limit; and turning profit. Upon his return to Norway, he had gained a reputation as a ruthless corporate raider in shipping, seafood, and engineering. He lived large, with a giant yacht and his own Boeing jet. But by 2003, he had nearly driven his shipping empire into the ground. Since then, he has sold the yacht, paid off his debt, and turned around his businesses. Of his business ventures in Norway, Røkke says, "Nearly fifteen years ago, I bought my first shipyard here in Norway. People were telling me, 'Why? Why do you invest in shipbuilding?' Financial advisors stated with confidence, 'If there is sunset industry, it most certainly is shipbuilding in high cost regions like Norway and Europe.' But I saw a potential they did not see. When I looked to Europe, I saw a highly unionized workforce, a highly skilled workforce, which made it possible for us to use the most sophisticated management tools; a broad cluster of equipment suppliers and technology providers; [and] innovative and challenging ship-owners."[72]

While Røkke's leadership style hardly is ideal, he exploits the ground conditions to the maximum, acknowledging that industry leadership starts from below, it starts with the workforce you have at hand. Røkke chose to build his business in Europe, not in the US, because of the highly challenging and dynamic workforce, even though it could be done cheaper or with less intervention elsewhere.

If you want to become a better leader, you need to expose yourself to complexity. It is easy … really. By tackling challenges and listening to people outside your domain, taking on new tasks, surrounding yourself with a multitude of people and objects, you will indeed think out of the box – most of the time.

Multicultural environments are crucial exposure. You need to observe, to meet and talk to the young, the old, and a mixture of social classes. You have to live in urban environments for a while; visit slums; spend time in the country, learning about farm life; visit other countries; talk to everyone you meet, strangers especially; and exploit serendipitous encounters. You will take every day on the job as a learning opportunity, constantly questioning what you encounter. You will have to get formal training on the side (MBA, courses, training, guest lectures, and conversations). Diversity is not something you are born with; it is developed through attitudes and exposure.

Other key skills and traits are empathy, integrity, and listening skills. You need empathy; through others, you can see the world more clearly. You need integrity; your leadership reflects who you are as a person. You will need to develop listening skills; to listen is the best way to grasp what is going on.

Leadership from below	Lesson # 11
Be aware of the worker's collective. Keep a healthy work-life balance. Work for egalitarian companies. Deal with diversity by exposing yourself to difference.	

Chapter 12

Online skills - making technology your own

Technologies develop quickly. How to keep up? By knowing just enough to break the rules and tailor them to your own use. And knowledge is insurance against surprises – as well as potential access to new markets.

I n the last few decades, office designs and the products we surround ourselves with at the office have changed profoundly. Telephones, computers, robots, and radios – change comes in many shapes and sizes. The technologies that shape knowledge work the most are small pieces of hardware, a few software applications, and the massive explosion in user-generated content – because they connect people.

Managing hardware

The most crucial hardware component is still the computer. Produced since the late 1970s, it has only been commonplace since the late '80s. The mainframe computer was at first mainly in use in universities and larger research labs and computer companies. On the other hand, the personal computer, an IBM invention soon to be coupled with a Microsoft operating system, quickly became more of a universal work tool. The laptop brought the computer onto trains, planes, sofas, and beds. There went all of our free time -- and some of our boredom. The pager, the cell phone, and the PDA further blurred the distinction between work and leisure, workplace and home.

Mobile phone technology has radically expanded the reach of knowledge workers and leaders. In the 1980s, even though cell phones were on the market, they were huge, cumbersome, and expensive – not really a mass-market item. Mobile phones didn't take off until the mid-'90s (first in Scandinavia, then globally a few years later) – but they are only now part of the American mainstream. Things take time. In the United States, the ownership structure for standards and airwaves complicated the take-up because it did not allow for easy competition across the country. Should you be a leader or a follower? A good rule of thumb: Technology is only worthwhile if you are the only one who has it or if everyone has it. That is, unless you want to take the risks inherent in being a trensetter.

Tools for information access

The Internet is used by more than one billion people.[73] There are billions of documents on the World Wide Web, only a fraction of which is searchable in Google. The rush to manage, organize, and search content will drive worldwide information access with search technology new license revenue to $368.9 million in 2006, up 10 percent from $335.4 million in 2005, according to Gartner, Inc.[74] Information access technology is establishes dynamic databases and search capacity in both structured and unstructured information.

Information access in business has become quite targeted. Assessing reliability is a huge concern, since input for decision-making must be as precise and updated as possible. You can now set certain preferences and let the search results show up in your inbox whenever you desire, using automatic search tools.

The information is coming from documents stored haphazardly on connected computers, from structured databases and from encyclopedias. An important emerging phenomenon in the last few years is the *wiki* – software that allows users to edit and post content on the Web, including the possibility to revise expert knowledge.

Wikipedia – people informing each other[75]

The largest collected work of knowledge in the world used to be *Encyclopaedia Britannica*. Nowadays, it is a user-maintained encyclopedia on the web called Wikipedia. The idea is that peer review nowadays should not be done by experts alone. Everyone should be able to influence the definitions with which we surround ourselves. You might say the wiki is leadership from below, par excellence.

The first wiki appeared in 1995, but wikis only took off in 2004. Wikipedia has more than 6,500,000 articles, including more than 2,400,000 in the English-language version that launched in 2001. All articles are based on contributions from several people, contain hyperlinks, and are available for editing by all users. Starting in 2006, users were required to register before contributing, but registration is simple and free. In a recent controversy, the journal *Nature* investigated claims that Wikipedia was inaccurate but found an almost equal amount of mistakes in paper dictionaries. The quality of information on Wikipedia varies depending on who has contributed to each article. Actors mobilize for their own causes. Concepts that are contested or popular are usually authored by many people. Wikipedia is a highly dynamic environment.

Search engines – Google and beyond

Knowledge workers spend hours every week searching for information. As the Internet evolved and the information available increased exponentially, so did the complexity. Not surprisingly, finding the right information became harder.

Search engines gained momentum between 1997 and 2001, trying to keep up with an ever-expanding Internet. Today, they are commonplace. But they have not kept pace with the Internet's expansion, and only a fraction of the Net can be "found" in a search. Search has expanded beyond text and numbers; multimedia search engines now increasingly find pictures, sound files, and such like Search is in its infancy, yet the search giant Google is now among the world's biggest Companies, measured by stock market value.

Search engines cater to many more than business clients. In fact, they are usually open to all Internet users. That is, they have been for some years -- namely, from the late 1990s until now. There has always been a price tag, but that has been taken care of by advertisers; in return, users have had to deal with the noise, commercial interference, and nuisance of advertising – and only occasionally reap the benefit. The provision of information is costly, and ownership of data is a valuable commodity. This has given rise to an information-access market for consumers and institutions. There are many reasons why user access to information is regulated. The government also continues to classify or just hide certain types of information, despite public information acts. Some occlusion is due to lack of communication between different technologies – so-called "interoperability." Governmental computer systems do not always talk to each other and are incapable of providing public access by design, even if government officials wanted to. To public knowledge workers, journalists, or engaged citizens, that is a growing issue.

There are currently hundreds of specialized search engines and a tenfold of generic ones. Yet the last few years have been characterized by the dominance of Google. In terms of presentation of information, we are now well beyond the lists of entries that we saw in the typical Internet portals in the 1990s. Already advanced visualization of various aspects of the information can bring semantic closeness based on similarity, history, reliability, or origin of the information. Context has also been refined. You can navigate based on location personal preferences, and within previously defined communities. Google "knows" where you're searching from. If you log into the search engine in Jordan, for example, your home page "becomes" Google Jordan automatically. However, search access is increasingly based on subscription fees. If that spreads to the rest of the Internet, "free" Internet may be marginalized and eventually disappear as quickly as it appeared.

"Free internet may be marginalized and may eventually disappear as quickly as it appeared"

For all the progress in the last few years, information access is still in its infancy. You still cannot find an answer to virtually any question by navigating in a global archive. There is no such archive, since the Internet only stores a fraction of the world's available information. On top of that, search engines only find a fraction of the information available on the Internet. Search-engine experts only find a fraction of that again. Ordinary people just operate on the surface. The role of meaningful, rich information (e.g., a semantic World Wide Web[76] with order and traceability of information) is generally poorly understood on the Internet. Now, most documents float freely around without being tagged with proper and secured meta-information about authenticity, authorship, origin, and date. Information production is still decoupled from information delivery. We still have a way to go from finding information to finding things and people. Future search engines will have to both allow us to specify (manually) and detect (automatically) patterns of relevant information. Following the development of information architecture and search technologies is essential to being on top of your leadership game. The way to do it is to read expert commentary specific to the Internet industry – usually found in good newspapers, IT-oriented magazines and websites – as well as the occasional book.

Leadership and search

When trying to educate about the Internet, high school teachers provide their students with ways to trace information lineage, currency, and reliability. While it is true that you cannot trust all information on the Net, there are indicators that help you assess the quality of what you find, such as: Is the information secure (by a person or an organization)? Does the website offer contact information for an editor or webmaster? Is the website owned by a reputable organization or brand? How recent is the information? Can you corroborate the information with different sources?

Search is not everything. You must know exactly what you are looking for. Otherwise, no search engine in the world can help you.

Screen technology

We are already surrounded by screens and display of every sort – large, small, and wide – and for more and more areas of our life. The only sure thing: Screens will become better, smaller, larger, and cheaper. In 2006, Parris Landing condos in Boston offered flat screens in the washroom. In airports, they are everywhere. They are starting to appear on public transport, in all waiting areas, in all rooms, and on all electric appliances. Mobile devices have smaller displays, more limited keyboards, and better pointing devices in comparison with desktop computers.

Computers and smarts

The fact is, computers today have a poor understanding of humans. Despite the fact that female users globally overtook male users at the end of 2005, programmers are still predominantly male. One of Google's hiring strategies for 2005 included calling up all graduating female PhD students from the top 50 universities worldwide and offering them a job. Times may be changing.

There are age issues as well. Most programmers are still between 15 and 35 years of age. When compared with the aging population facing Europe, for example, that hardly is sustainable, given what we know about the importance of user-centric software development. Before the age of 15, children are in school or cannot work too many hours due to legal and cultural restrictions. Yet we know that children are huge users of information technology, from computer games to email, messaging, and online communities. After that, they either end up in leadership positions, or they are sidestepped, change professions, or otherwise disappear from software development. Why this reference to child labor? Well, in principle, toys should be developed by kids, just as users should influence the products they use. Only intense user-involvement can ensure fit between users and products. But when will new technology emerge without these flaws? At the very least, children should be involved in product development focus groups. Turning the trend of non-involvement of children, women, and senior citizens will take some time and the speed will depend on how demanding new users are.

Email – a killer application

Email has been available in universities since 1970s and widespread since the 1990s. In 2008, all knowledge workers use it. However, email is only effective if you know how to use it. Early email systems were configured to send research findings between scientists. It started out with words alone; no formatting or fonts were available -- and certainly no pictures. Large files, what we now call "attachments," were sent via a separate system.

Very few product developers foresaw the social usage of the last decade. This teaches us a few things. Firstly, be careful about predictions! Email will change. At any time, there is a set expectation -- in the office, by your boss, among the technical staff, and from the email provider -- about how you should use email. Beyond that, you can stretch the functionality in several ways to make it more tailored to what you want to do. Nowadays, there is choice in the marketplace. There are free and paid, basic and advanced services -- the choice is abundant.

Email competence, however, has mostly to do with communication. The old rules apply: Know your message; try to figure out how it will be received; and tailor your message accordingly. Also remember that since you are not on the other end when the delivery happens, you do not know what state of mind the other person is in -- or who else may be reading it. Your email could be forwarded as part of a joke to a third party or will be used as leverage against you or the institution you work for.

Email usage has evolved from the 1970s (when it was primarily used by programmers as well as the military), to the 1980s (when it entered academia), to its mainstream usage in the 1990s – during which the medium has gone from informal to formal. Email is now official, both in government and in the private sector -- meaning there are lawsuits connected to them. In fact, informal communication is now largely moving to messenger systems and online communities, where you can control much more who receives the information and where forwarding often is not possible. It seems people prefer built-in safeguards to maintain the informal nature of electronic dialogue.

Social networks

On today's Internet you can keep in touch, play, and visualise their own perspective on the world through online communities like Facebook and YouTube. You can network with peers in business communities like LinkedIn, Plaxo and Xing. As an employee, you can build corporate community in intranets. I participate in a dozen of these, and I have created a professional best practice community for European stakeholders in e-government (epractice.eu). My experience is mixed. Community is hard to create, hard to sustain, and definitely very easy to destroy. But when they succeed, they can be immensely powerful – although usually not for the purposes they were originally designed for.

Common to all of these, is that they build on the natural inclination of people to respond to social cues. Now, it may be useful to keep superficial contact with lots of connections, cleverly called "friends" on many of these online sites. The more pressing question when you try to use it to get real work done is – will these ties respond to more serious requests? More often than not, the answer is no.

So, the real warning here is not to get too excited. You can rely on people you rely on in the real world. You can get to know them better through networking sites. In fact it may even build relationships – given that there are enough compelling reasons to do so. But the Internet does not create wonders. People do.

There may also be thresholds to look out for. There is a proliferation of community sites and community development these days. But people's attention span is limited. People's patience with being your online helpdesk is limited. How much is too much community?

What the Net can't do

Current trends lead toward a proliferation of technological objects that affect leadership, although not always for the better. Mastering changing conditions demands a command of the underlying logic. Leaders must have realistic expectations and experiment as well. While technologies like the Internet are powerful, they will not transform society overnight. In this chapter we have looked at the mastery of technological objects. The most efficient way to perform knowledge work is to apply the principles of leadership from below.

Get an active relationship with technology; try to understand more about your implicit assumptions about how it contributes to, may interfere with, or could enhance your work:

Identify your total leadership environment. Look at your own immediate surroundings, your office, the infrastructure in and around it, the city you live in, the objects that are of potential use to you or your colleagues. Are there any missing? Should you introduce new objects?

Re-think your own use of technology and other resources, like office supplies. Are you using them as intended? Or, are you using them in your own way? Are you using objects for what they are worth? Overriding user scripts can release innovative potential – so be creative. Figure out whether you have any particular experience or aptitude to "sell" regarding their use.

The way office technologies and objects interact, how well they are handled, what infrastructure is in place, whether they are fit to purpose or merely disturb the flow of communication – all of this affects their efficiency for the knowledge worker.

Interestingly, even the ancient technologies can contribute significantly to innovation. They are not saturated or beyond their best days yet. There was something so fundamental about them that it will take a long time to change. Or their legacy is so entrenched that we refuse to do away with them. We have become dependent upon them. In fact, we are comfortable with them in our culture.

Feeling comfortable with a technology takes time. The telephone, which was invented by Alexander Graham Bell in 1876, did not take off immediately. In fact, 130 years later, some people prefer not to use it for sensitive communication. But it is certainly preferred to the computer for those matters. A European study found many prefer the phone to the Web when interacting with the government on sensitive matters.

In the end, your choice of technology remains influenced by many factors outside of your control. You have to consider whether your employer is supportive of your choices. Even armed with a memory stick and portable applications, using technology that nobody else in the office is using is not necessarily fruitful. It creates distance between you and them; does not allow you to fully be in sync with their needs, worries, and concerns; and could, therefore, turn out to be counterproductive. On the other hand, as long as you select carefully, being at the technological edge could give you the advantage you need to excel. The choice is yours.

Leadership from below	Lesson # 12
Choose a few knowledge technologies – such as online communities, email, and a PDA – and ignore the rest. Master them, go beyond their intended scope.	

Chapter 13

Really being heard

Stein is a business developer for an investment firm specialized in green technologies. He could pick up a stone from the ground and sell a treasure. In fact, he has done so since age twelve. In his family, stories and unique collectibles are held in high regard, but stories are held even higher. Emerging leaders who know how to present themselves and their message outdo those who do not. If you present well, the subject matter is less important.

The essentials of public speaking are easy to master. They involve practicing confidence, knowing your material well, and having all available tools at hand. You must practice public speaking regularly to hone your skills. In the beginning, you can start by speaking out loud, rehearsing your presentation in front of a mirror, a tape recorder, or video camera. Leaders from below treat every time they speak as a presentation of sorts. Thinking this way is good practice. The three components of your voice – tone, rhythm, and volume -- must match your audience.

A ballpark figure often quoted by books on presentation skills is that around 40 percent of what you communicate to others derives from the way you say things, 50 percent derives from body language, and only 10 percent derives from the words you use.[77]

Presentation is about preparation. Keep past presentations (as well as your other indispensable documents) on a USB flash drive – carry it with you at all times. Make sure you have relevant objects, technologies, and people at your fingertip. Then do all the thinking, research, and reading; collect experiences and catalogue stories to share. Remember that the clue is always to have the audience with you, following your thoughts, being surprised, being carried along. You may think of some preparatory instructions or "homework" tasks for your upcoming audience – email it, call them up, send a paper, have them bring in stuff. Think about the way you will convince people, whether you will use graphs, photos, or other quantified or visual evidence. Spend some time on the presentation tool, but never too much. The rest is best spent rehearsing.

Presentation software – Slides and beyond[78]

Presentation software is a persuasion technology that typically includes three major functions: a slide-show system to display content in a linear fashion, an editor that allows text to be moved around en masse from slide to slide, and a graphics system for quickly drawing charts and graphs. Replacing earlier technology like whiteboards, slide projectors[79], and overhead projectors[80], presentation software enables you to show your ideas in digital form.

When presentation software started to become commonplace in the 1990s, there were not many products on the market. At first it was used to generate black-and-white pages that a photocopier could turn into slides. Soon, it was used in combination with a projector. Microsoft's PowerPoint, launched in 1987 for Macintosh and in 1990 for Windows, quickly became the predominant visual presentation application and has dominated the market for well over a decade.[81]

According to its vendor, Microsoft Corporation, some 30 million presentations are made with PowerPoint every day, and it was shipped with almost all computers made from 1990 through 2008. As the name indicates, the software enables you to make powerful points -- but at the expense of depth of detail. The richness of the longer memo, speech, or paper is constrained into a ten- to 50-page bullet-point presentation in which the rest of the content is presented orally. Information presented by slides may be forgotten or buried the audience's notes and thoughts. Despite these shortcomings of contextual clarity, the technology has been immensely successful.

What is the psychology behind it? Why is it so successful? As most of us know, PowerPoint can be a good way to mask ignorance – the software is that good. Interestingly, the creative team behind PowerPoint was known for their independence, fiercely defending their invention for cutting the middle man – the designers – in favor of content and core message. Nowadays, this is precisely what PowerPoint is criticized for: streamlining ideas that previously were presented in naturally flowing prose with complex arguments and using a personalized style of delivery. One reason behind this change is the AutoContent feature, added in the mid-'90s to provide "ideas and an organization for your presentation," according to the instruction manual. Now there's an array of template presentations (including graphics) for every occasion, modeled on earlier lessons from American public-speaking books a la Dale Carnegie's *How to Win Friends and Influence People*. Thus we find "generic" presentations, "recommending a strategy," "communicating bad news," "training," "brainstorming," etc. These templates will, of course, structure your ideas and improve the clarity; but they will also change the content of your message, because the original narrative is lost.

"The advantage of slides is clarity, brevity, and communicability across contexts"

The anti-PowerPoint movement[82] dates back to the early 2000s. In 2003, Edward Tufte wrote an influential essay called *The Cognitive Style of PowerPoint*,[83] in which he argued that the tool draws attention from the message and toward the medium itself, as well as toward the speaker. In contrast, key tenets of the Asian Zen aesthetic are simplicity, beauty, grace, and visual elegance (*kanzo*), which are best achieved by elimination and omission, trying to achieve maximum effect with minimum means.[84] The risk with PowerPoint is that subtle ideas become sloganized, simplified, and corrupted; they become commercialized and may sound like a sales pitch.

"Slides can never fully convey context, meaning, or process"

The other, more subtle issue is that your own medium – your body, your voice and body language -- is in competition with more and more animated, colorful, and catchy words on ever larger and translucent screens. Sometimes that is a bad choice, especially if your voice is powerful or you have a compelling visual presence.

Thirdly, using slides removes a key part the thought process. When delivering a PowerPoint presentation, you can skip the reasoning and follow the bullet points directly to your facts, findings, or conclusions. Often, too many bullet points are used, so even the utility of clarity and concision is lost. In short, through a company's monopoly, a software product has shaped the thinking and speaking patterns of people across the globe. Today, the emerging OpenOffice software suite contains presentation software (Impress)[85]. The program, which is not fully compatible with the dominant program which is Power-Point, suffers from a lack of ready-made presentation designs, although third-party templates are readily available on the Internet. Its key advantages over PowerPoint are (a) that it is distributed under an open source license and is, therefore, free for most users, and (b) that it is based on an open standard.

So who loses in the slide society? I would say, the storytellers, the poets, the critics, the individuals, and the ones interested in learning, context, and meaning – many people lose out. Slides can never fully convey context, meaning, or process. It is an impatient medium for peoplewho lack voice, poise, and presence -- or someone who doesn't have the time for a more meaningful, in-depth message.

You may, of course, always combine your own power with PowerPoint. By pressing "B," the screen goes black, and you can regain control for a minute. Pressing "W" will return to the presentation. Very few people know this simple function.

An alternative or a supplement to using presentation software is holding up real objects – nothing can substitute for a full-bodied, fruity bottle of 2004 Cabernet Sauvignon wine from Napa valley, a sweet, fresh orange from Jaffa in Israel, or a bloody, red piece of filet mignon from Argentina.

Personally, I tend to use slides for most presentations, but I skip it for personal, literary, intellectual, or emotionally charged occasions (e.g., if you are trying to discuss something -- not just present it -- or if you know the subject matter by heart). The point is that presentation software is merely a medium. The script says we should use it a certain way, and, while we master users may overturn it, we're not always effective. Use whatever gives you the most momentum.

How to use slides[86]

Leaders make conscious decisions on when and how to use presentation software. Is it fruitful to what you are trying to accomplish? Will it get your message across efficiently?

Do not waste your time trying to make the perfect slide. Your time is better spent thinking about your ideas and message – letting assistants, offspring, or even designers take that part of the job – or just keep it simple.

Sometimes company policy dictates when to use templates and what we can write on a slide. Follow policy, but don't become a slave to it. *Creative opposition can be smart.* Complement the presentation with a different medium handout (for instance, a plain text that summarizes the points or provides more of the context). Do not overwhelm the audience with high-tech effects, sounds, and moving images. It distorts their attention to the message.

Think about colors and font size; adjust content to the audience. Generally, headlines should not exceed two lines. Twenty-point font is the smallest you should use. And, always cut 20 percent of text when you think you are done. Avidly use common abbreviations, key words, and never full sentences. Try to use the same color for the same "concept" or domain throughout. It is a mnemonic tool that works.

Presentations are speeches to be performed -- not read, not rushed through. Despite powerful IT tools, you may need to practice and question what you're saying. You may also need a second or third opinion on how you are doing.

Engage with your audience from a variety of angles. Surprise them. Presentation software may enhance presence, but it may also hinder it. Make sure you know the difference, and study your effect on various audiences; experiment with all of your repertoires across the settings that confront you as a knowledge worker.

Slides are of little use without a screen on which to project it. Sometimes your laptop screen is sufficient; but with an audience in excess of five people, you need a digital projector[87] to display your presentation or videos on a wall or canvas. There are a multitude of decent products on the market, but it is still prohibitively expensive to own your own (happily, this will most likely change within the next decade). Thus, for now you at the mercy of the conference organizer, your own employer, or your rental options. The important thing to remember is to have a back up (e.g., hard-copy handouts, your own laptop screen, or old-school slides or overheads – which would be quite nostalgic). As with other technologies, you will have to weigh the importance of purchasing a projector for yourself or your employer. You may find it's worth it, at least if it is portable.

Leadership from below	Lesson # 13
Master presentation skills first; then master content. Use slides wisely and sparsely. Perform; do not read your speech. Rehearse – and get feedback on your performance -- beforehand.	

Chapter 14

Developing presence

Leadership is about being present in the situation, making your self relevant. Presence is also a balancing act; you can't be too pushy or too passive. You must use all available means, combining your online and offline repertoire. Activate the people you have met and trust: your community of practice. Watch situations evolve and react quickly.

Not only must a leader have the capacity to read and speak well, but also she must be able to express herself clearly in writing. While the skill may still be performed offline, there are considerable benefits to using a blog to get better organized and solicit feedback from readers.

A Web log or "blog" is an online diary – a personal website in which you can write or present digital files on whatever you want. But bear in mind that what you write can be read by anyone with a computer and an Internet connection: Most blogs are on the open Internet. That means they are searchable. However, of the tens of millions of blogs out there, only a fraction are actually read by many people, although readership is on the increase, as well.[88]

Leadership from below means expressing your opinion in public often and earnestly. You need the feedback to be a good leader.

- Regularly send a piece to the op-ed column of a newspaper;
- Send newsletters to your constituency, whether they're customers, donors, members, or peers;
- Send a memo to your boss every month suggesting changes, addressing issues, or updating him on important developments in your field.
- Start a blog and contribute weekly (or more)

Multi-sector mindset

I have started my own company; worked at universities, think tanks, and international governmental organizations; and conducted fieldwork in large high-tech companies. What strikes me most about the variety of my former workplaces it is that, at first, each seemed totally different from the former -- until I moved on and could see it more objectively. When you are inside an organization, you easily become myopic. You see nothing beyond your own situation.

Management consultants are usually good at quickly grasping an environment's challenges. Some firms develop their consultants as generalists who can work with any business and in any sector, but this is not always the case.

While you may study multi-sector dialogue and partnerships through courses at the university, it only gets you halfway. You also need to experience it. In terms of formative professional experiences, you should try to gain experience from industry, as an entrepreneur, in public sector, in NGOs, and in large international organizations. Rapid job shifts will have a price, but, for your own growth, two years in each place is optimal. Before that, preferably in college, you should try to have a couple of internships and overseas sojourns. Since you have to mix and match, you may have trickier job shifts, and this is a riskier approach.

Call on your community of practice

It is important to understand your own network. What resources do you possess, can you mobilize, or do you otherwise have access to? What capital (financial, human, symbolic, or other types) will they require and, thus, what it will cost you? Already Dale Carnegie had understood this, with his bestseller *How to Win Friends and Influence People* (1936). His advice was to always speak in terms of other people's interests, to know what they like and give it to them, to say their name as often as possible, to know what and whom they care about, and to give sincere praise. He had a point. However, what Carnegie and others did not mention is that your community and surroundings also include important non-human objects, such as computers, mountains, coffee shops, and the like. They are also epistemic resources; that is, they can help you be a better leader and knowledge worker. In short, you need to understand the completeness of your surroundings, what they contribute on the whole, and what each element can do. This is most apparent when there is shortage or scarcity. Imagine being stranded and alone on an island and needing to make do with what you have or can find. But it is equally pertinent if you want to be innovative, do new things, and change the world. Every new idea makes you a loner -- until you have convinced someone it makes sense.

To a certain extent, you can influence your surroundings. You can move around, choosing to spend your time in particular locations, with particular people doing exactly what you enjoy doing. Of course there are limitations, such as the need to earn a living, concern for family, health, the remoteness of some of your favorite places, and so on.

Most Nobel Prize winners (in physics, chemistry, physiology, or medicine) have previously worked with a Nobel Laureate.[89] One could argue that the best way to win a Nobel is to find a laureate and become his apprentice. Well, there are no guarantees, and the selection process among apprentices of top academics is fierce, but there is a point here. Even though one can stumble upon excellence and creativity anywhere, the only way to be sure is to go to the places where the excellent and creative hide. If you work next door, you will miss out on the ecosystem of thoughts, practices, and resources in the most unique research labs and universities.

Research also shows that identity is at the heart of knowledge work. You will perform better if you identify with the task. For that to happen, you need to believe in it, have a supporting network around you who also do so. The network needs to be sustained over time. Surround yourself with people you trust, derive competence, opinions, knowledge, and resources from them, discussing their point of view.

Successful knowledge workers bring their professional connections when they change jobs. In fact, they bring with them a core group already from college, or even before that.

I keep a journal where, from time to time, I make small illustrations of who matters most to me, both personally and professionally. Mapping out friendships and other relationships this way is a way to self-calibrate and to focus on what's important to you. Otherwise, in a fast-paced life, it's hard to focus on what matters and easy to just go with the flow. The small illustrations are never fully complete, and they change with time, mood, and circumstance, but this little exercise can be fruitful. You may discover that you have not been in touch with even your closest allies, friends, family, or important network connections.

This exercise may result in a greater understanding of your weak ties and who in your network can help you in a particular situation. It can also help you to be systematic about whom you keep up to date with.

Get to know yourself better

Who you are, your personality, the basis of your integrity, your fundamental beliefs, your formative experiences (everybody has had fundamental experiences or have been in dramatic situations that have shaped them) -- all of these are important for leaders to think through. They lead to acting a certain way, an image to whom others look, and they are the source of your financial, symbolic, and cultural capital. In other words, they are important to your leadership, since they provide your starting point.

You always need to be realistic and honest about your own potential, assessing your own qualities and faults. Make sure you are the one person who knows yourself the best -- otherwise you may get into trouble. If someone knows more, they can exploit it. More importantly, if you do not know yourself, what you do might harm you.

One of the best ways to develop self-knowledge is by keeping a diary, something I have done for many years. They provide a common thread to which you can refer back when in doubt about your own feelings or what you have done -- or when trying to decide what to do. They document the flow of time through your own emotions. There is no better map than that.

Find balance with family

The domestic nucleus -- spouse, immediate family, and close relatives -- is important to your leadership, since, with them (hopefully), the essentials are discussed. They provide a base of emotional support and guidance, equally important in times of crisis and success. Ignoring this part of your life will not make your leadership sustainable. Family relations are tricky because of your history together; nevertheless, you should always try to figure out how to relate to them, both privately and professionally. How can you ensure they add energy, rather than tap it from you? What have you shared together that is relevant to your professional life?

There are always lessons to draw from family experience. Family can be a great source of wisdom; they can help you understand others and yourself. You will be surprised at what kind of advice you get if you consult a family member, rather than a friend, colleague, or mentor. Your family's advantage: They know you well; they (generally speaking) want the best for you; and they never go away. Their disadvantage: They never go away. Remember that.

Get experience from all sectors

Governments are traditionally hierarchic and bureaucratic – which, in theory, means that authority lines are clear and that every inquiry is treated fairly, providing public services to all. This leadership model is under pressure, and it is also not always clear for outsiders – citizens, business stakeholders, customers, or consultants – exactly how to behave. If you know government from the inside, you don't have that problem.

Business is virtually impenetrable to a person who has spent his career in nonprofits or government. Top business jobs are mostly passed along through networks, the performance criteria are different, and the work is different. Learning to have a customer focus, to work efficiently and concentrated – in "the zone" – are things you can learn in business that can be applied elsewhere.

Nonprofit charity organizations have traditionally orbited in their own galaxy, separate from the public and private sectors. The insight it takes to find a job at a charity remains hidden to those outside it. Nowadays, as governments and business contract with, deal with, and sell to nonprofits regularly, failure to understand their operating logic will lead to many misunderstandings. Nonprofits may be challenged by the fact that a significant part of their workforce is unpaid, part-time, or underpaid. In this sector, leadership requires a different approach when motivating employees; teamwork must be very flexible to cater to the fact that the leader has little or no resources to offer beyond pride in the product or belief in the organization's purpose. Traditionally, leadership skills, as well as accountability, have not been high priorities. But this is changing. Stakeholders are putting all organizations under pressure to be visionary, transparent, and effective. Nowadays, many nonprofits could teach big business a thing or two about social responsibility – and transparency.

International organizations tend to be amorphous, with diffused authority, complex networked relationships, and multifarious conflicting interests. They also tend to be very hierarchical. Leadership here is similar to that of governments, but cultural differences and a lack of purely democratic accountability increase complexity. Nongovernmental organization experience offers a multicultural repertoire from exposure to diversity.

Try the teamwork approach

Most people do not realize just how many teams count them as a member. Today, teamwork is everywhere. Make sure your core teams at work and in voluntary organizations include peers, adversaries, and strangers. Make sure you are involved with a diverse group of people. Know your role in relation to the task; know the stakes; and always prepare a unique contribution. If you are uncomfortable with what is going on, reassess your role or quit. The key is to prioritize. Never expend energy on something unless it has real meaning or value to you or to the community to which you have chosen to contribute.

Be a good colleague

Proximate colleagues whom you meet face to face every day, in the canteen, in the elevator, at the coffee machine, copier, entrance, meetings are your most direct source of wisdom, assistance, and comfort -- but also frustration. They will see you on good and bad days. Make sure you give them your best, even on bad days. Drop a joke as often as possible. Think about them both in terms of what they care about at work and elsewhere. Follow up with encouragement. Be on friendly terms with people at all levels of the hierarchy. Administrative assistants can be the best source of insight on an organization; do not underestimate them.

Nurture friendships

Friends are important to your leadership because they define your emotional bandwidth. Whom you interact with, in a certain sense, is who you are – the definition of your personal boundaries. Your friends define what you talk about, how you may present yourself, far beyond your image to the outside world. Make sure you have the friends you want to have, who give you what you need. Make sure you are a good friend, and to the right people who deserve it. Friendships are rare; those that last are even rarer -- and they are a source of great strength. They also need to be built, maintained, and challenged from time to time, in order to maintain their vigor. Who are your good friends? Make sure you are happy in this arena of your life. Otherwise, your knowledge work and leadership will suffer.

Meet your mentor

Everyone should have a mentor. If you don't, find one. Mentorship can take many forms – formal, informal, implicit. Peer mentorship is also possible. The important thing is to have people to guide you. They are sources of peripheral legitimate participation. They give you access to experience, advice, and encouragement that you might not otherwise have. After all, you cannot live several lives. Talking to your mentor is a way to test the water, ask questions, be honest, and get advice that saves you time and mistakes. She or he could be professional, personal friend, friend of the family, or even a soul mate.

Capitalize on your contacts

Most people have a larger network than they think: Generally, each of us is a member of between ten and 30 associations. First, figure out who your contacts are, how many you have, and what expertise or life wisdom they represent. Then, make sure you keep up with them regularly. Establish a way to stay in touch with a lot of people. Make your own list of Platinum, Gold, and Silver contacts – and reward each group differently, as do credit card companies. How much credit do these people have with you? Do they deserve more or less? You can send Christmas cards, call them on their birthday, or send small updates on your professional or private life as appropriate. Make sure you have all the contacts you need for what you want to do -- not just now, but also in the future. Be open to letting other people show you why they are relevant to your life.

Find your platform

Your "platform" is slightly distinct from all of the above. It may be related to one or several of your key people or networks. Essentially, a platform is the position from which you can credibly address an audience, whether online or offline. It may be your unique experience, aristocratic family (lucky you), looks, skill-set, political connections, media access, your own website or company, op-ed skills and contacts, political party affiliation and status, size of your employer. You will get nowhere without it. Without any of the above, get creative. How can you make your experience more unique.

Make an overall evaluation of your life; make sure you keep it up to date and change approach if you feel you are getting nowhere. You may even ask, "How can technology help?" Create your personal CRM system, mapping relationships, their function and meaning, how elements interact, sources of strength, figure out where you are weak, divide into overall resources, and niche specific resources.

Tailor your challenge to the environment

Already a pragmatist, psychologist John Dewey (1859-1952) determined that experience, interaction, and reflection are keys to learning.[90] Knowing the local conditions may provide knowledge about whom you can bother and when. Proximity gives you the opportunity to observe people, their moods, business, interactions with others, actions, behavior, and insight into local routines. Used well, you have an ability to intercept people who are working on something else without really disturbing them. This is the power of your informal presence. If you have compelling ways of doing it, you can stop people, pop in and out of their office, mention things casually, and then follow up.[91]

Challenge people within their proximal zone of development:

[T]he distance between the actual developmental level as determined by independent problem solving and the level of potential development as determined through problem solving under adult guidance, or in collaboration with more capable peers. (Vygotsky, 1978).[92]

For leadership from below, it means that you should only give advice to peers or provide input to superiors that is within their sphere of comprehension, and just slightly outside their current outlook, perceived scope of action, and meaning. Too far out, too creative, too innovative, and the take-up will be low; your thoughts will be perceived as irrelevant, incomprehensible, or out of scope.[93]

Proximal development implies that the role of experience is fundamental to leadership: Your approach will be effective only if it touches previous experience of those whom you are trying to lead. It means you need to know your environment and the people involved; try to understand their concerns and their experiences (at least their key ones) in order to tailor your input.

In her 2004 book *Confidence: How Winning Streaks and Losing Streaks Begin and End*, Harvard scholar Rosabeth Moss Kanter mentions inclusion as pivotal to industrial leadership. This is interesting, because inclusion is an issue for governmental digital divides and democracy debates; working toward inclusion is fruitful for leaders, because it creates confidence and winners over time. You must include everyone, or else they will sabotage your efforts. And sometimes performance depends on the weakest link. Other useful lessons from government-type cogitation include:

- Thinking in terms of the common good (not just wanting to look good in front of your shareholders, the next customer, C-level executives, your immediate boss, and your colleagues);
- Contributing to job security and stability in people's lives; and
- Ensuring fairness and access to services for all.

Psychologist Howard Gardner shows that diversified learning is needed; there may actually be multiple intelligences at play, each with separate working profiles and learning styles.[94] Challenging experiences force people out of their comfort zones. Leaders actually try to create a sense of disequilibrium, causing individuals to question the adequacy of their present way of thinking.

You cannot ignore the culture of the place where you work. You need to make the organization your own, capitalizing on its strengths, and minimizing its weaknesses. But while organizations differ, you will always benefit from maintaining strong links to the outside world. And you also need to fit in with your customer; consultants spend more time here than anywhere else. Become an accepted insider, no matter what your organization. And keep your outside ties – all successful leaders and knowledge workers do.

Organizations differ. Fitting in and being productive does not mean the same in the U.S. government as it does in the United Nations, the European Union, a Norwegian software company, or a Bhutanese farm. As a knowledge worker practicing leadership from below, there are some lessons to keep in mind:

- Watch what others do. Being in sync with insiders breads familiarity and acceptance for you and your ideas.
- Know the reward system, both formal and informal.

- Treat everyone with respect, from the administrator to the C-level executive.

- Be genuinely interested in others. You learn more and people will like you.

Privileges

You should keep a good work-life balance. The balance may shift during different phases of your life, depending on whether you are single and hungry to succeed in your career at all costs, or you just got married or had a child and want to have time to the family, or you have other family issues to deal with, such as illness or loss. You may also actively engage in spare time hobbies; take time out to travel; and to experience and savor all life's pleasures. In fact, a healthy balance between work and leisure is essential to a sustainable career. Remember that you will work for many, many years. With a global increase in retirement age on the horizon, you will most likely be working well into your seventies, regardless of which country, private retirement scheme, or employer you collect benefits from.

When at work, make sure there is enough time to rest your brain cells and refuel your energy. Take short breaks at least every three hours. Get enough fresh air. If you can, you should walk, skate or run for 45 minutes at least two times a week. Use a refreshing workout to socializie and wind down. Spend time with people with whom you need a good relationship.

To succeed in life as well as in your work, you need to have a spiritual balance. Whether you seek that balance through yoga, meditation, holy books, scriptures, spiritual retreats, or religious services, you cannot perform at your best without recognizing that life has a deeper meaning. Having a value system helps you to focus -- to decide what is important and what is not.

"Knowledge workers need praise. Set them free. Constrain no one, and you will be successful"

Take charge of your immediate environment. We have talked a lot about the various objects that may surround you in a typical day. Some of those objects are imposed by others and will not disappear. Others you can choose. Do not carry a cell phone if you can avoid it. If you must own one, make sure your employer pays all the calls, including private ones. Establish limits for when you must be available. If someone demands full availability, you should be compensated for that. Your time is valuable. Interruptions are costly both in intellectual and emotional energy.

Demand flexible work hours. Work from home whenever possible. In fact, apart from a possible minimal common time for meetings, preferably in the late afternoons in the middle of the week, you should have no requirements to be anyplace at all. All should be left up to you and worked out directly with those whom you work with, whether they are projects, teams, clients, or what have you. In fact, whether you carry out the necessary work in one or in ten hours, one or ten days should not matter to your employer. Knowledge workers should not be paid per hour but, rather, should be compensated for the value they add to their employer, to society, and to themselves.

For all the intensity and peak experience they crave, the new breed of leaders want to have balanced lives. One way to keep all of this in check is to maintain a diary of your own major emotional and knowledge triggers -- almost like a set of bars or meters, expressing where you are every day and every week on the scale. Only then can you really assess what is going on with your life. Soon there may even be software on the market to monitor this progress: project management for one's self.

Leadership from below	Lesson #14
Be present in the situation, activate your community, and stay grounded.	

Chapter 15

Networking government

Leadership in the public sector may be the hardest of all. Traditionally, there are few incentives to perform, plenty of incentives to maintain the status quo, and many barriers to evolution. Recently, this is changing. Awarding excellence in government is on the increase. Networked bureaucracies are, bar none, the strongest organizations.

Governance increasingly depends on social networking (whether or not it is conducted via the Internet). Stakeholders demand more and more attention, and transparent consultation processes abound. In Europe, there is even a formal name for it: "the open method of coordination." But in Brussels, the capital of the European Union, the 3,000 journalists and even larger number of lobbyists create an environment in which special interests rule the scene. Washington, DC, is much the same.

The consequences of networking within the government hierarchy and especially between government and its stakeholders (citizens, business, NGOs, etc.) can be more openness, transparency, and communication. Citizens' concerns may matter more. Business concerns may make or break a legislative proposal. However, networking may also mean chaos. The problem is that it challenges the current model of government: that of representation.

Networked governance refers to trying to institutionalize working with networks, understanding and embracing change while keeping the best of the legacy past.

Beyond bureaucracy

By its very nature, the public sector resists change. Bureaucracies were designed to evolve slowly. Their goals of efficiency, transparency, and equality, while admirable, are not easy to act upon. Their sheer size, complexity, and diversity, governed by hierarchically, are part of their historical heritage. But society is changing. And while the process of governance increasingly depends on networking, governments are still managed from the top down. Yet, as a policy response in the last decade, we have seen the emergence of networked governance -- that is, trying to institutionalize working with networks. Do civil servants cope with this new environment? What are the issues they encounter, using information technology systems, institutions, and skill-sets that handle public policy challenges, staying both resistant to pressure and yet embracing change? How can knowledge workers who interact with government succeed?

David Osborne and Ted Gaebler's bestselling 1992 book *Reinventing Government: How the Entrepreneurial Spirit is Transforming the Public Sector* advocated, foreshadowed, and actually inspired trends like entrepreneurial, mission- and customer-driven, market-oriented government. The book became a bible of the Clinton administration. The public sector is by no means unable to reinvent itself. But there are so many ideas on the market and no reason to jump on all the fads. Also, government cannot and will not "jump". It is institutionally embedded in both its history and culture.

John W. Kingdon[95], a public policy scholar at the University of Michigan at Ann Arbor, USA, first described the phenomenon of policy windows, when things can suddenly happen. Policy windows open only briefly, and enable civil servants or politicians to launch their proposals, either as part of the budget cycle, or through regular reports or addresses. A scheduled renewal of a program is another example. Windows open infrequently and stay open only for short periods, and all who want influence must rush to take advantage. Just as surfers float until the right wave comes along to start paddling, so too do lobbyists and politicos, lying in wait like lions before their prey.

Successful bureaucrats show persistence. Kingdon cites an informant who says: "A strong senator is one who is just there. He is willing to be at the meeting." Aside from being there at the right time, in order to be somewhere relevant when a policy window opens, you need brokering skills and the willingness to negotiate your position.

The public knowledge worker

The work practices of civil servants provide the context to which all eGovernment initiatives must relate. In what way do they face the developments of networked governance? Do they enjoy it?

Civil servants embody their institutions. Their common ethos through the history of their institutions, in some sense, "is" the institution. Thus, they take on the public memory, classification schemes, and decision-making process of their institution. Leaders of government represent both their own policy and the legacy of their supporting civil servants. Civil servants operate within institutions that were designed to evolve slowly, so as not to jump on to every fad or seemingly smart idea. The institutional focus on efficiency, transparency, quality, and equality -- the embodiment of traditional bureaucracy -- is not easy to modify. Their sheer size, complexity, and diversity are part of their historical heritage. In theory, public administrations are controlled by authority as exercised through hierarchy, even though newer approaches advocate bottom-up and local control, responses that better match administrative practice. Understanding how to deal with those two trends has proved difficult. One study found organizational factors such as social networks, reward systems, and information and communication technology (ICT) deployment have a significant effect on knowledge sharing.

Demographic characteristics in public institutions vary greatly. But since they mainly were built after World War II, the aging of civil servants has become a big issue. Recruitment of new blood is attempted and is often quite successful. Training programs and career/leadership development programs for civil servants have recently been put into place in the United Kingdom and Ireland, and traineeships for young civil servants exist in Norway. What these programs have in common is that they try to prepare people for change, to supply them with a variety of skills so they are universally employable across institutional boundaries. The most forward-looking nations also encourage or even facilitate cross-sector exchanges throughout their career.

But what if civil servants try to be different or enter the workplace with a different mindset? What happens then? How does the environment meet them? Is there room for pockets of inspiration and innovation within public administrations?

An example from real life: An official in a European administration was instructed by his superiors to send a letter by the close of business. The letter was to include signatures from one level up the ladder, but it also required comments from that level. After an initial phone call to an assistant at the next level of the hierarchy, they agreed to proceed as follows: The official would first send an email to all parties involved, explaining the urgency and requesting final comments on the letter. The email was sent, and things seemed fine. An hour later, a secretary rushed into the official's office saying, *"This is a bit embarrassing. We need to recall your email."* The official, perplexed, asked for an explanation. Well, the secretary said, there are procedures to follow. You can't just send an email when you are communicating with one level up the hierarchy. We need signatures on a physical dossier before we can send any communications, especially since you wanted several high level people in the hierarchy to sign the letter. It turns out she was responding to an email from her counterpart -- the secretary of the person who had received the email.

This secretary had not been in the loop about the initial discussion highlighting the urgency of the letter. She was more concerned with proper procedure than efficiency. Eventually, the whole issue was resolved by creating the physical dossier and sending it around for all parties to sign, a process that could take a week or more. Yet, somewhat mysteriously, the letter went out that same day anyway.

This example illustrates the tensions inherent in going toward email-based communication or, rather, combining email and paper flow. Understandably, there are routines to follow. But there are also questions of what makes the most sense to do. If some quick comments are needed and an email is the quickest medium, it tends to be used a lot, even in public institutions.

While all email may be archived on servers and theoretically retrievable, mostly it is not categorized in traditional ways and used as formal communication. Rather, it is something different. Email usually takes a place as informal messages part of the daily workflow. But it can be highly effective and save taxpayer's money.

Now why did some parties object to the practice of emailing first, then sending the paperwork? Apparently, it was because there was little precedence for this approach, at least not documented or available to the ones who objected.

New entrants immediately face the pressures of "how institutions think" and learn "how we do it here." After initially observing internal practices, having dealt with the consequences of doing things differently, experimentation often stops -- and the civil servants are socialized into status quo.

Bureaucratic procedures were invented to ensure fair and equal treatment of people, cases, and documents, regardless of the bureaucrat. Bureaucrats are supposed to be interchangeable. They should all proceed in the same way, safeguarding equal treatment of all issues and avoiding preferential treatment. Obviously, that puts bureaucracies at a disadvantage when it comes to customer service. They cannot provide *superior* service to a select few but, rather, guarantee *good* service to all.

The future of government

Today's eGovernment tools, including workflow and presentation software, present challenges to the old paradigm. By presenting new opportunities for communication, they in fact tend to "destroy" hierarchies. No surprise, then, that many, especially upper-middle management and occasionally secretaries tend to object. They lose control with what is going on. Information flows toward their counterparts without them knowing. There is a multiplicity of ties, both within and outside of the institution that provide input to the leadership. In every deployment of eGovernment (if it has any effect at all), the role of management will change. It may be that some tasks are done differently, but it does not necessarily mean less power to management. Rather, wise managers (public or private) efficiently adapt to eGovernment by flexibly figuring out how they can carry out their mission with their new role safely in place.

We have said eGovernment tools tend to destroy hierarchies. But will this really work in the long run? Is there a possible backlash? After all, when strong people see they are loosing the grip, they try to counteract. In fact, in one public administration where I once worked, a higher official made it clear that he wanted to see all correspondence, even emails, before it reached the minister or his advisers. He got his way in the beginning, but the practice was frustrating to many. It created extra work, slowed things down, and did not necessarily improve the quality of advice. Why? Because quality lies not in the number of layers or people who have seen a document but, rather, in whether those people provide a value-add. The official had tried to twist the script of the email technology too far. But email is easier used, and more sensibly used, as an informal tool. Too many people use it informally for one official to change the momentum.

If we examine these two examples, the paper dossier and the incensed high-level official, there are some striking differences compared with the way things occur in industry, First, very seldom is there a paper trail when matters are handled in-house; second, power struggles tend to manifest in much the same way. There is little change there. Bad leaders are usually bad leaders in any context. But when it comes to the way to handle a bad leader, there are many more options. The consequences of being a whistleblower are lower, especially if the team agrees. Then the leader is replaced rather than the knowledge worker. Civil servants, on the other hand, tend to have their job for life and can, at best, be placed elsewhere on some special duty.

But both government leaders and their civil servants have to keep the warning about the nature or knowledge workers in mind. While you cannot ignore them, their most radical attempts to work anywhere, anytime (nomadic work) will most likely not work at all. Certainly not for managers who want a minimum of predictability and control -- or those that want to ensure creative team processes.

While it is true that some processes were reengineered, mostly by adding ICT to the equation, we are neither paperless nor nomadic, either in government or industry. It was simply too hard. Or, one could also argue, it was the wrong target. It turns out there is a benefit to showing up to work. The face-to-face encounters enhance the pitching and subsequent "freezing" of ideas necessary for progress in any organization. Government and civil servants in particular simply cannot be only online. They have to meet – among themselves and with the public.

All of this goes to show that change is good, but not when it's untamed. Domesticating technology and change is essential, especially in the public sector. To achieve this, there is no way beyond worker buy-in, culture-aware management, proper motivation, and long-term perspective.

Today's public-sector knowledge worker should be aware that embodied knowledge can be effective. While a lot of effort is expended teaching management, less is spent teaching how to be a knowledge worker. Yet this is trickier. It involves a trade-off between following the wishes of the hierarchy (which variously may mean expedient, predictable, short-sighted, or rash) and going for networked (often common sense) solutions that could be more effective and fun -- but also time-consuming, because of all group and individual exchanges. Public knowledge workers face this challenge every day, and there will not be an easy way out anytime soon.

You cannot change civil servants in an instant. You cannot change institutions. You cannot change the technologies. These things evolve over time. And sometimes incremental change is more sustainable than the sudden, groundbreaking revelations. Many of those, such as the perennial "paperless office" idea, have taken us 30 years to implement; it will take another 30 to see its fruition in government. Involving users (citizens, civil servants, agencies, and industry); adapting to its own needs; setting requirements for technologies and, thereby, domesticating change, therefore, is especially essential in the public sector. It is essential that civil servants enjoy networked governance. For the moment, they are mostly exposed to it at the fringes -- flirting with it, so to speak.

If you work in business and deal with government, you need to figure out where your counterpart is in terms of this evolution. Try to see yourself and present yourself as an extended advisory board to a particular initiative. As long as you do not claim to know better how to run government (which you do not) but, rather, only claim to have specialist knowledge relevant for the impact of ideas or proposals on the table, you will be considered relevant and non-threatening. Officials like to surround themselves with that type of business advisors, as long as the role is clear and nobody steps out, crossing the fine line between influence and corruption.

Loosening hierarchies

In the 2004 book *The Future of Work*, Thomas Malone writes about how businesses like Google are loosening the hierarchies, working with flexible projects, with few management layers, reading each others' blogs, without the need for top-down direction. In this book, I have studied leadership from below principles which are based on the same logic.

Similar processes are starting to emerge in governments, distributing the responsibility for carrying out public services to private actors, but keeping a monitoring role. So-called services for public interest include hospitals, welfare provision, and schools. Public-private partnerships are another way hierarchy is loosened, and governments now share responsibility for budget, delivery, and service quality with private or nonprofit entities. Involving stakeholders deeply in policy consultation is another way to share responsibility. Writing blogs would be to go further along this line, and it is happening to some extent -- although many officials are weary, and those blogs tend to be anonymous. The paradox is that the more power government gives away, the more it gains in terms of credibility. The European Union, for instance, is often criticized for its democracy deficit and needs to go further down this road.

The future probably has room for it all – hierarchies, networks, and governance. Counter intuitively, governments and civil servants can attempt networked governance, leading this change by active policy choices. Or they can leave it to industry or to the inevitable organizational "gut reaction." Either way, despite the promise of the Internet, eGovernment projects, and networked governance, the most likely turn of events may be scenario two: status quo. The co-existence of hierarchy, bureaucracy, and networked governance enabled by technology will continue to challenge efforts to put citizens at the heart of public services. After all, civil servants, their leadership, and even citizens will do what is best for them and will not wait for the ideal solutions. Are you a good servant if you agree to be socialized into status quo?

Leadership from below	Lesson #15
Governments operate with hierarchies in place but allow networks to co-exist, trying to strike a balance. Respect and play their game. Find policy windows and wait for the right moment to strike.	

C hapter 16

"No meetings, please"[96]

Software companies are notoriously difficult to lead, since programmers are fiercely independent. How to reconcile business and pleasure? How to motivate co-workers?

C harles Simonyi, father of Xerox's groundbreaking 1972 Bravo X program for the Xerox Alto computer and coordinator for Microsoft's development work on Word and Excel, once said:

> *Programming is art, just like high-energy physics is art ... actually, it is a mix of science, art and skill. ... [T]he first step in programming is*

imagining. ... I try to imagine the structures that represent the reality I want to code.

What Simonyi said is that programming evades description (which is hardly a good start for us who are trying to do just that). But it's exciting nevertheless.

We are not the first trying to do this -- hacking the hacker, as it were. What we know is that all programmers are driven by the desire to develop code. The computer is their canvas, the software and its lines of working code their visible result. Embedded in this notion is an almost fundamentalist ideology that information should be free at all costs. Although not all computer programmers today feel this way, the powerful Open Source movement has roots in the computer science departments of the 1960s and 1970s. It is historically accurate to say that after an early dominance, it was weakened during the 1980s reign of IBM and then under Microsoft in the 1990s. But it has picked up the pace again.

In the last few years, Open Source has received massive attention in the computer industry. Larger corporations embrace Open Source as a way to organize differently, with less bureaucracy, and sound knowledge-sharing routines and practices. To some, it is also a way of pointing toward a company culture in which raw talent and peer-to-peer evaluation is valued more than traditional networking with the leadership.

Opentech – high tech with a twist[97]

Working on this book, I did extensive fieldwork in a Scandinavian software company we can call Opentech, founded in 1996. *"We were four people in one room who were just having fun. I don't feel like it was work at all,"* one of the founders told me. Another said that the team programmed until they were dead tired, then downloaded their new software to a place called Sunsite, and then we went to bed thinking, "Tomorrow, we will post a message saying we put our program out there." The next morning, there was an email from Australia: *"Cool program, just what I've been waiting for. Only one thing, here's a patch that should constitute a new class needed."* The show had begun. The Australian guy became employee number five. Recruitment to Opentech continued this way in the first years. Many employees have autodidactic careers, based on intrinsic motivation, inspiration from a larger group of insiders, and watching and practicing with mentors.

Opentech employs several hundred people from some twenty countries and has several offices around the world. They are an example of a company practicing leadership from below.

When Opentech employees start, they get a collection of three papers by Eric Raymond on Open Source software as an ideology and programming style and four books. The first book, *Peopleware,*[98] by Tom Demarco and Timothy Lister, reads as an anti-Dilbert manifesto (for those who are familiar with the cartoon about boring office work). *Peopleware* is about how teamwork in software development feeds on a process called flow – being "in the zone" or concentrating without interruption. The second book is Geoffrey A. Moore's *Crossing the Chasm*[99], which deals with selling high-tech products to mainstream customers – a challenge when the company itself comprises first adopters with radically different outlook and needs. The third book is Donald A. Norman's *The Design of Everyday Things*[100], a seminal work on user-centered design. The fourth book is Frederick P. Brooks's *The Mythical Man-Month*[101], debunking the myth that if you add more programmers to a late software project, they necessarily get more done and recuperate the lost time. The reason they won't is that it's necessary to communicate more (i.e., network ties take time). The overhead increases as well.

All in all, quite a reading program! Now, why this gift? According to the CEO, these books reflect the personal inspiration of the founders -- the thing they have cared the most about in creating Opentech. Let's look, for a moment, at the impact of *Peopleware* on company work practices.

Flow – the key to knowledge work

Peopleware is about creating a workable environment for programmers, allowing them to work in natural light (all offices have big windows), avoiding a perfectly uniform space, and letting them shape the space to their own convenience and taste. Big, dedicated working space gives rise to productivity, and top performers' space is quieter, more private, better protected from interruption. And there is more of it. Top performers tend to gravitate to companies with ample working space.

The work also presents the concept of flow. During single-minded working hours, employees are in what psychologists call "flow" – a condition of deep, nearly meditative involvement (i.e., unaware of the passage of time, euphoric, unconscious of effort. It takes 15 minutes before this state of mind is "locked in." By the way, flow is not required for all work. The challenge is the following: The concentrated state of flow can be broken by an interruption, a phone call, a noise, or a voice calling you. Yet the only thing that matters is uninterrupted work time -- not the number of hours you are physically at work. As one Opentech programmer told us: "Code is ready when it's ready. Deadlines are stupid and an obstacle to developers."

What effect have these books had on Opentech? Do the employees read these books and articles? Do they agree? Do they use their insight? Have the founders succeeded in creating a company culture that nurtures exactly these and not other values? In 2002, the answer was yes, but things change.

Let's go to 2002, where the physical setting at Opentech is as follows: two floors, both equally shaped in a long corridor that gets wider as you go along, with big doors and glass walls toward the corridor (some of which are covered by posters or book shelves, thanks to programmers who detest being looked at from the outside). The design of the space is classy and their own; There are two programmers per room, all of which have closable doors, big windows with suitable sunscreens at their own choice. There are large desks, top computers, new, slick office equipment, good design chairs, and white boards in all rooms.

In *Peopleware*, the hatred toward telephones is pronounced. This is directly reflected at Opentech. Phones are seldom used, except among sales people; there are few loud sounds and extremely intensive use of online and SMS text messaging. My expectation of a nerdy crowd was initially rewarded: It seemed electronic communication ruled. But the impression did not last. The social dimension took me by surprise with a comment made by an employee: "We are not sitting around the same lunch table anymore" (i.e., they are spread out between lunch tables in Oslo, Brisbane, Santa Clara, and Beijing).

The importance of the lunch is only matched by the impact of the silence. An almost solemn silence resides in Opentech at all times, except on the hottest summer days, when people run around for lack of better strategies to survive without air conditioning. The respect for the software developers is astounding. First of all, they are called developers, since software is taken for granted. Due to the importance of flow, nobody is allowed to interrupt if it's not crucial to the ad hoc practices of the programmers themselves. It turns out they are incredibly social, popping up in each other's offices all the time, asking a question or two, sharing screens for a while pondering a problem, or just chatting about tech issues they care about. Written communication (email, Intranet postings, ICQ, fixed-phone SMS) serves as the everyday, routine-based flow of impressions. But the oral culture is dominant. Such a work culture relies heavily on informal chats during lunch, in the hallway, and serendipitous encounters.

Egalitarian leadership – leading through example

At Opentech, there is no use of titles in internal communication. The Intranet directory has no indication of corporate rank, only phone numbers and brief task descriptions. Office doors only have names, no titles. After a month at Opentech, I hear the story of how the signs came down after a week or so. A temp office worker tried to introduce titles to simplify things, but massive protests arose. The CEO took charge after a week, and tore down the signs himself. The purity of peer principles is holy in Opentech – but you need to be a programmer to be a peer.

Programmers do their best work when they do what they want to do, not what they are told to do. Occasionally, there are boring tasks that just have to be done. These are distributed across the organization. The HR director told us the following:

"Things become too ad hoc sometimes. Customers propose some things, it seems interesting, and we [look into it]. We might find out it's even bigger and ask who wants to contribute. But unless our programmers want to, we don't do it".

Both naming and gaming are important here. Playing around, playing table tennis, soccer, or Nintendo – a "troll" (as they call themselves) just wants to have fun. That is, in between the intensive work sessions. But being serious programmers, they subscribe to hacker culture. Trolls read science fiction and fantasy;

are fascinated by technology also on their spare time, though not exclusively; and many of them have elaborate hobby activities.

With such shared identities, proximity knits workers even closer together, and distance becomes problematic. For instance, one guy – let us call him Jim – who works remotely from the Netherlands thinks it is problematic not to be there physically. He can concentrate well at home but can't go into a coworker's office to ask about things. Also, his emails need to be reinforced by a phone call. Other people's emails count more than his. This can be frustrating at times.

Opentech meeting culture reminds me of a student organization – chaotic, pragmatic, and unorganized, although somehow effective. Yet, as the months of fieldwork unfolded, the very practice of meetings is problematic here. There was a company story behind that too. But what about contact with customers – how they talk about them, approach them, find them, hold them, or keep them?

Again, in 2002, customers were mainly approached by email. But it was already starting to change. In 2005, the entire approach to sales has changed, and they have become a more traditional sales organization. Their Web page is visibly more streamlined in outlook, less "techy," and catering to a more mature, non-technical audience of C-level executives. Some employees among the original ten have already left the company. New executives have entered the scene. By 2008, the company is arguably a global player. In fact, they have been acquired by a multinational player.

Running a business with no meetings

But what about the effect of the *Peopleware* philosophy on core business: programming?

An Opentech programmer explained his motivation:

I am never bored. I rather have to be pushed to go home. Time flies. My primary motivation? Being able to work on a product that is so free [like our program X], you can bring in yourself so much. We have no real conditions from the outside. ... So I don't have the feeling that if I fix something or write something new, that it will vanish somewhere in some proprietary product of Opentech. ... But we're free, as long as we're still making profits with it.

Opentech programming culture, in fact, tells you to interact without meetings. After many frustrations among his programmers about the increase of company meetings, the CTO emailed everyone a five-page document arguing that Opentech could eliminate meetings altogether:

Meetings are useful to exchange information, to distribute tasks nobody wants, and to do decisions that require majority votes. They might be useful to generate random ideas for long-term strategies, provided you have enough time and not enough plans for the future, but I doubt it. Deep talks of few individuals over a couple of beers combined with thought-through written proposals via email are certainly more efficient. Either way, meetings are a bad instrument to get work done. ... In the development department, we basically only have informal meetings between those who are actually involved in the specific project, and only if there is really an issue that needs to be resolved. In other words, we do not have meetings at all, but fellow workers talk to each other whenever this is needed.

The CTO's email, written in response to Opentech management's questions about development culture, led to a decrease in meetings -- but not a complete cessation. The company has since been acquired by a larger player and is likely to change significantly. That company does have meetings.

Professional tensions within a firm

In a software company, professional identities co-exist. Managers and programmers do different things, think differently, and live differently. Managers might be former programmers or recruited from the outside. In any case, they have longer experience and oftentimes a higher salary than programmers. They are in a tight spot, trying to lead programmers whose credo is peer-to-peer exchange.

Professional differences or, rather, the way they are handled may lead to a lack of understanding of each other's roles and competencies. In some ways, this also means separate business cultures (based on education, work practices, and lifestyle); they interact only on need-to-know basis because of few contact points. Of course, one of the reasons why they don't interact directly is that there are many more programmers than managers. A completely united culture might be hard to achieve. Secondly, there are status issues. A lot of the trouble arises from salary envy, titles, compensation, and recognition.

It would be too easy to write off these tensions as purely related to the fact that managers organize while programmers code. The real conflict lies deeper. One manager said the following:

Programmers have been crucial to our business and have always had the lead role in our company. The first five years of our existence, programmers handled all tasks, including sales and marketing. So the first employees tend to view this job as a simple one that doesn't require a separate set of competencies. I guess, not as important of a job as programming either. Developers don't like all the manager titles on the non-technical side. Actually, those on the non-technical side sometimes give the impression that they feel like secondary class citizens. Now we have to prove that sales people are not interchangeable.

This conflict, while as deeply rooted as the one between managers and programmers, could possibly interrupt an otherwise effective high-tech company. Being aware of the problem may not solve it, but could assist in this process. Professional competence struggles involve the structuring and usage of the information systems powering the high-tech work place. Salespeople, for instance, tend to have little patience for restrictions on what programs they can upload to their computer, what file formats are used to send attachments, etc. To programmers, on the other hand, such choices are the foundation of structured and professional work practices. Managers sometimes do not see all IT systems as a strategic issue and leave it to the chief technology officer (CTO) to figure out. The problem is that IT impacts work practice in a very deep way, especially in a software firm.

The traditional conflict between the interests of managers and software programmers is highlighted in Open Source companies like Opentech. Even when recruited from the same pools, managers and programmers do different things, think differently, and live differently. Their choices make sense within their own rationale. Managers are interested in moving projects forward, taking the lead on new initiatives, following up with internal and external clients, establishing and meeting deadlines and constraints imposed by leadership or outside environments like customers, competition, or business partner relationship dynamics. Managers, of course, are primarily interested in management. Programmers, on the other hand, are interested in coding, peer review of their own and contributed patches, working toward the perfect running code based on shared consensus, competent user feedback, and challenging coding tasks. Their main arena is the written code, and they prefer to work uninterrupted by non-programmers. Programmers, of course have the main interest of programming.

The following observations are applicable whether you are leading a company with more than 1,000 employees or a company growing beyond the important 100-employee mark. In both cases, the critical communication between managers and programmers should be monitored and facilitated in subgroups of 70 to 100 people who should form some kind of community of practice.

- Observe, document, and monitor the growth of programming culture, as well as of product manager culture in your company.
- Regularly communicate your survey findings.
- Try to maintain close physical proximity between programmers and managers, yet not too close not to prohibit or inhibit self-expression.
- Educate product managers on Open Source culture; convey the respect required to work professionally.
- Let programmers join sales training; hire a tech-savvy sales force.

What can we learn from this? Well, certainly that the face-to-face issue is complex. Some companies attempt to solve everything online, but nobody completely succeeds in doing so. Opentech does not even try. What flows naturally online is treated as an online problem; what does not is immediately recognized as a problem of a completely different nature -- something that demands face-to-face attention. This could be, for instance, an innovative idea that needs to be discussed, strategic meetings that involve negotiations, or important customer relations.

Open Source and proximity

Regardless of Open Source principles and practices, physical proximity (at office, company, city and national levels) shapes specific organizational trajectories. In fact, the Open Source community, and online proximity as such, only accounts for one among several crucial determinants of knowledge-worker performance on the company level -- even among fiercely Open Source-friendly firms. The national research and development (R&D) system and innovation cluster also has a significant impact on how a high-tech firm works, organizes, and executes its strategy. Thus, Open Source never seems to occur in a virtual vacuum but is, rather, a complex, integrated, and physically demanding practice, as well as a networking enterprise of gift-givers and honor-seekers – all of whom are opportunists, idealists, and pragmatists.

It what way is Opentech a virtual corporation? Obviously, a great deal of activity is coordinated online (e.g., queries, billing, and shipping by downloading rights, etc.). High-tech work is complex and hard to describe. Hacking, or experimental programming, goes on by way of binary coding, algorithms, and computer languages; it also occurs as face-to-face discussion and straight talk.

In Opentech, high-tech work is occurring at its technical extreme end. On the other hand, as we have seen, the extremely low-tech strategies of eating lunch together to establish common ground, or just popping into each others' offices when you have a question, exists peacefully alongside. We counted nine such spaces with impact on the work flow:

- Work space (two-person team offices) for programmers and sales staff.
- Meeting space (a lunch room, a library, and one dedicated meeting room).
- Social space (a terrace, a lunch room, a table tennis area, a kitchen area).
- Office space (national, regional, local, floor).

- National space (Norway, Germany, the United States, Australia, Asia)
- Global space (the Open Source community of several thousand programmers as well as the market they operate in).
- "Non space" (large hallways) to create isolation; strict silence is enforced.
- Low-tech spaces of flows (phone, fax, cell phone, letters, memos).
- Secure e-space (Intranet and internal email contact).
- Open e-space (Internet and external email contact).

The relative importance of each space and the work practice associated with each is hard to assess without giving an example. Right before a major product launch the focus is intense. In fact, innovative activity only takes place when all of them come together and gather momentum – what we previously have referred to as *hyperspacing*. Tentatively, we may say that despite the hype of online practices taking over, both the social and non-spaces seem key to Opentech organizing. Conversely, the hyped up face-to-face meetings might not be all that important when they are all about communicating ongoing initiatives, unless the message is controversial, complex, or employees need to be convinced, motivated, or controlled.

There were obvious differences between the knowledge works of distinct groups of workers. Senior leadership (CEO, CTO, HR) preferred offline encounters among themselves, since issues are complex and debates over strategy need face-to-face attention; yet they might cleverly use online communication to spread simple information. Product managers achieved a lot by checking progress through lunch comments but were the big Intranet users. Sales preferred low-tech communication spaces achieved by phone, mobile phone, and fax, while programmers coordinated most work through email and IRC, combined with casual encounters in the hallway and occasional intense teamwork sessions. In fact, during my time there, Opentech experimented with so-called "extreme programming."[102] In this method, all code is programmed in pairs, and only that pair integrates code at a time. All programmers were assigned a buddy, and each pair had their own office.

But what does observing this company tell us about knowledge work and leadership from below? Several major findings can be highlighted:

- Organizational culture is liked to the configuration of communicative spaces. Some were designed, others emerged.

- While Open Source prescribes programming practice, its entry into the management of organizations is more problematic and leads to organizational tensions.

- The road from a garage culture of a fresh start-up company to a transformative culture at 100+ might be described as a molding process, in which knowledge workers undertake structuring work.

In the typical garage stage, everyone (mainly computer programmers) is on a first-name basis; they eat lunch together and are, largely, a company of friends. In the typical corporate stage there is a strong company brand in place. Workers have a corporate identity, a fixed place in the hierarchy, and are motivated on a frequent basis by speeches from its charismatic, yet remote leadership that spends most of its time outside the customers doing PR -- investor, media and customer work. Employees work in equal cubicles and avidly defend their company's principles and practices if challenged by outsiders, whether friends or competitors. A company may reach the brand stage before hitting

5,000 employees, but it is unlikely to be able to sustain itself as a global brand for very long, since that requires momentum – in customer base, sales, advertising, and visibility. Nokia became such a brand with its "connecting people" ads in the late 1990s.

As of 2002, Opentech is somewhere between the two extremes, with a community-based identity of shared meaning and belonging common in religious congregations and strongly knit together cultures.

"Programming is a social practice. Management always fights a battle for programmers' loyalty – which always lies with the code"

The rules of big business – and breaking them

In 2002, the law of large numbers started to hit Opentech, having hit the 100-employees mark, rapidly advancing toward 150. From a programmer's point of view, someone will have to do the boring stuff. There is a larger need for organizational coordination, bureaucracy, and repetitive work. The idealism of the founders and first employees meets the professionalism of the new hires.

Structuring work is a necessary part of Open Source, rather than a peripheral, imposing constraint. There are obvious ways to handle increasing complexity and obvious challenges to the paradigm. For example, Opentech has:

- Adopted a slightly cultish company culture based on values from the Open Source community, yet largely adapting the external rhetoric of conventional high-tech firms.
- Imposed daily rituals that reinforce this shared culture (e.g., free lunch at noon).
- Required a minimal dress code – casual and easy, but dressed up when meeting people from the "outside."

- Building a transparent intranet with open access to budgets, customer information, and incoming corporate email.

- Moving as slowly as possible toward the near-inevitable corporate culture that follows the initial garage culture of enthusiastic entrepreneurs.

These practices have emerged both because of pressure from the outside world and as a result of dynamics in the company culture itself. The downside of this strategy of playing along is lack of focus. The company might spread itself too much and might try to make everyone happy at the same time. There is no doubt that ad hoc adapting is among the risky business strategies. On the other hand, for Opentech, the alternative is to break the code and go completely corporate. In fact, as it appears, Opentech anno 2002 had to make the choice. Stay small and keep the culture, or keep growing and possibly loose what is retained from the informal, garage organizing principles established by the founding community. But on the other hand, Open Source itself is changing with the tides. A wise company experiencing growth should keep the following in mind:

- Inform employees of the foreseen changes going on in the organization.

- Legitimize changes by illustrating how they will improve working conditions for all the involved parties.

- Be proactive about change, but only when change is needed.

Structure is only good if it solves a pressing problem. Free spirits might not work better under these conditions, and some will find better things to do if structuring work becomes a burden.

Motivating high-tech workers

Motivating employees in more mature companies is not only about the intrinsic motivation of getting to submit clean code and taking the responsibility and credit for it. It also has to do with internal pride, weighing the work of programmers versus the work of sales and product management. The cure for the necessary conflict between management and development work practices can only be found by deploying swift, yet light leadership. It is important to steer, not to lead in the strict sense -- to guide rather than to instruct, to motivate rather than to impose. The company culture of Open Source companies seems to be an extremely vulnerable thing that needs to be cared for and nourished regularly, just like other good things in life -- like relationships, cars, and pets. And that might be the most valuable lesson of all.

Leadership from below	Lesson # 16
Being in a state of flow is to concentrate so that nothing else matters. Let flow be a part of your workday. Have empathy with other work styles. Take pride in your own ideas. Strive to be recognized for what you do.	

Conclusion

To engage in leadership from below is to ground your leadership in the here and now. It includes being aware of Asian principles like ba, Zen, feng shui, kanso, and ki and following Scandinavian egalitarian, collective, open, and gender-neutral practices, working both with network and hierarchy, flexibly adapting your way of thinking, acting, and "placemaking" to the surroundings.

Leadership from below is the motto of a new generation of knowledge workers. It originated in Scandinavia in the 1960s, was kept warm in teamwork throughout the next decades, exploited by entrepreneurs starting up new companies in the 1980s, gained speed in the Internet's way of facilitating networked relationships from the 1990s, came to fruition in the Open Source movement in the 2000s, and will likely emerge strongly in the coming decade as the awareness of energy flow (Ki) is growing, also beyond Asia. The generation that has experienced most of these phenomena was born between 1970 and 1990; they are now between 18 and 38 years old and will influence the world in unimaginable ways into the twenty-first century.

A new generation of leaders is being bred – one that favors freedom, free flow of ideas, and access to information. Why not combine online and offline activities, skills and strategies? The knowledge-worker lifestyle merges job and play, home and work; is mobile, yet connected; nomadic in reach, but rooted in reality. There is no such thing as work or free time. All is fused in the knowledge lifestyle. Leaders and knowledge workers are geared toward the personal, emotional, and intelligent peak experience. Leaders improvise and make life work.

Managers who deal with this new generation of knowledge workers have to invent new ways to lead, motivating them to work; to come in to the office; to report to a leader; and to work with a deadline – all of which may not be their centre of attention.

Whether you work in an ideal organization that supports your growth or you work in a stifling environment, you can do something to improve the situation. But context matters, and all management advice, even with the leadership from below perspective, must be applied with care. People respond differently to the same conditions, and no situation is exactly the same. Therefore, one must experiment to find what works. The important thing is to have the confidence to try, the persistence to keep trying, and the heart to tackle the new environment if you succeed. There are two things emerging leaders should be doing; they seem to go in opposite directions: *exploring* (traveling, gaining experience, seeing things for yourselves) and *staying rooted* (in your community, being loyal to your values). In reality, one can indeed do both – and one should.

The leadership from below paradigm goes like this:

- Be prepared. Re-think all your formative experiences, so they can work for you not against you. Read everything you can get a hold of on your possible topics of engagements. Never stop learning. Immerse yourself in what you do, so it becomes second nature.

- Know your place. Do not try to be a leader if you know you are not able to contribute. Do if you are. Leadership from below comes from inside, yet you should consider what other people say about you as well. If you have heard other people say you are a leader, you probably are.

- Assess the situation using your own "compass." Know what is going on both in the small and big pictures. Know why your co-workers act as they do, or try to find out by asking them or just observing them. Handle your boss. Always look good in his eyes. Do what makes sense in that total picture.

- Act on your instincts and have confidence in yourself, especially when you have faced similar situations before and, in fact, know what to do.

While sociological and management knowledge can empower and prepare people and their organizations for change, there is no such thing as an experiment or a book that will prepare you for the real thing. The network society has to be lived – thinking, pushing, pitching, -- building teams, using the flows of globalization to change things by employing leadership from below. It is all related, the flow of globalization, the state of sustained concentration that psychologists call flow (and athletes call being in the zone), and the energy flow that Eastern thought calls ki. The important thing is to remember to be grounded, using the forces of gravity, of grounded action, to motivate our struggle. Placemaking consists of making all forces work together.

But do not wait until you are at the top. Most will never be. And once there, ideas will have burned out, or will no longer matter. Ideas are now. As the examples have shown, it is worth it to apply the principles of leadership from below now, not later.

Glossary

Short definitions of about 50 key terms used throughout the book.

Action research: A blend between consulting and research.

Capital assets

> **Economic capital:** money and assets
>
> **Social capital:** people, skills and networks
>
> **Symbolic capital:** degrees, affiliation, brand, reputation
>
> **Physical capital:** infrastructure, strength, surroundings

Ceremony: A gathering that serves as reassurance and reminder.

Company stage

> **Garage**: 0-99 employees

Transformative: 100-199 employees

Enterprise: 200+

Brand: 5000+

Corporate: 10,000+

Cyborgs: People who are enhanced by technology.

Egalitarianism: A democratic, open culture.

Encounter: Brief, casual face-to-face contact.

Domestication: Making an object or a process your own by changing its intended use.

Explicit knowledge: Has a clear meaning across contexts.

Globalization: An increased flow of people, ideas and technologies across borders.

Hyper-spacing: Putting all online and offline resources to use, convincing others and engaging in place-making.

Ki: Awareness of the energy flows that surround us, which will make you energetic, alert, and powerfully present if you pay attention to it. Ki deeply resounds across cultures and is similar to what westerners call intuition.

Knowledge work: Two types of activity, isolation (thinking, and concentrating) and socialization (pushing, and pitching).

Leadership from below (LFB): A management perspective whose premise is built on peer-to-peer principles, community, and social, physical and psychological balance and eastern principles of energy. LFB is based on transparent and widely communicated values.

Leadership senses: Sight, Hearing, Taste, Touch, Ki, Intuition and Proximity.

Legacy environments: The physical infrastructure and objects that remain important and cannot be wished away, such as large computer systems (even if installed long ago).

Management: A discipline based on achieving results based on clever use of hierarchy, command, accountability, knowledge and control – technique.

Meeting: A discussion to reach consensus.

> **Meeting technology:** Online enhanced multimedia, video, or whiteboards

Momentum: Strength or force gained by motion or through the development of events. Also called "snowball effect" or "network effect".

Open source: Programming practice where the key asset is free access to information embedded in software code.

Placemaking: When we take in the impressions around us and make them our own. In business, we can use this to our advantage when we negotiate, speak and present.

Place-presence: When you physically interact and this has noticeable effects on facts, feelings, actions and situations.

Policy window: When a change of political winds suddenly opens up for new initiatives.

Power-presence: When you physically interact and this has noticeable effects on facts, feelings, actions, or situations

Presentation: The pitch of an idea or a concept.

Proprietary: Programming practice where licenses with strong Intellectual Property Rights (IPR) protect the code.

Proximity: The richest communication possible between people. Proximity builds on face-to-face and body-to-body relationships and triggers trust, respect, and intimacy.

Screens: Symbolic representations of life and work.

Script: The visible and invisible instructions for use, built into an object. There are often tensions between an object and its user, who may want to override the script.

Significant others: The people who mean the most to you, defining your identity.

Strong ties: The people you know well and trust.

Successful team: A group whose elements (e.g. people, process, leadership, and resources) lead to deliveries beyond initial expectations.

Tacit knowledge: Cannot easily be expressed. Everyday practices of people whose routines, thinking patterns, activities, words, texts and actions become taken for granted.

Team: Twelve or less people working together for a limited time to achieve common goals.

Team roles

>**Assigned leader:** Formally in charge

>**Informal leader:** Takes charge

>**Social leader:** Steers with strong emotional intelligence

Devil's advocate: Argues against the consensus

Team proximity

Virtual teams: Meet and communicate electronically

Face-to-face teams: Meet physically

Hybrid teams: Meet online and offline

Virtual presence: When you successfully simulate presence through technological means, creating some temporary form of virtual reality.

Weak ties: People who you know of, who know many people whom you do not.

Worker's collective: Loyalty between workers against management.

About the author

Trond Arne Undheim is a leader, entrepreneur, speaker, and academic. He has co-founded several start-ups including a think tank and his own consulting firm. He obtained his Ph.D. (2002) in Technology Studies and Sociology from the Norwegian University of Science and Technology and lives in London. For a full biography, see: http://www.linkedin.com/in/undheim

ndnotes

[1] Power distance is a notion developed by political scientist Hoefstede in order to account for varying degrees of distance between political leaders and citizens in different societies.

[2] Technologies have politics. The expression derives from the work of American scholar Langdon Winner, see "Do Artifacts Have Politics?" in Daedalus, Vol. 109, No. 1, Winter 1980. Reprinted in The Social Shaping of Technology, edited by Donald A. MacKenzie and Judy Wajcman (London: Open University Press, 1985; second edition 1999).

[3] For a timeline of events, see http://thinkprogress.org/katrina-timeline

[4] The notion of tacit knowledge was first explored by the philosopher Polanyi back in 1966.

[5] The French sociologist Pierre Bourdieu was among the thought leaders of the 1990s bringing the notion of embodied knowledge back in to social science. He built on French philosopher Merleau-Ponty who argued body always expressed our perception of things around us. For more insight, see Bourdieu (1996) in the bibliography.

[6] A full theory of knowledge work is found in Trond A. Undheim, *What the net can't do*, Trondheim, Norway, 2002 [Ph.D. thesis], available in full text at: http://www.hf.ntnu.no/itk/ikon/tekster/Undheim_STS55_2002_NET.pdf

[7] The first to popularize the Japanese philosopher Nishida's notion of Ba was the Japanese management scholar Nonaka in 1996.

[8] Source: IBM Global Innovation Outlook (2004).

[9] Castells, 1996, op.cit.

[10] Our inspiration for the place making theory is found in the works of classical sociology, especially Durkheim (1911), as well as the French phenomenologist Merleau-Ponty (1945), and the contemporary scholars Latour (1999), Hannerz (1992), Bourdieu (1996), Lie & Sørensen (1996), and Berger & Luckmann (1967) as well as among Gestalt psychology theorists of sensory perception who discovered 'insight' learning. A more elaborate version of the place making theory is found in *What the Net can't do*, Trond A. Undheim, STS-report 55, Trondheim: NTNU, 2002, the Ph.D. thesis of one of the authors, op.cit.

[11] *Built to last* by Collins & Porras, 1994; *Good-to-Great* by Collins 2001

[12] For more illustrations of how technology is introduced into everyday life – and domesticated – see for instance Silverstone 2000; Sørensen 1998; Undheim 2002 in the bibliography.

[13] Louis Pasteur, lecture 1854. French biologist & bacteriologist (1822 - 1895).

[14] The American psychologist Robert Cialdini claims that influence can be obtained through seven different techniques: We can give away something or return a favor (reciprocity). We can show that we believe in something and are willing to go far to defend it (commitment). We can show that others are doing it (social proof). We can play on our good appearance, on similarity between us and them, give compliments, breed familiarity, condition them to associate us with something they need (liking). We can appeal to a higher power (authority). We can appeal to the fact that what we offer is hard to obtain (scarcity). Finally, we can try to hit psychological triggers in people's mind, things to which they have long ago developed a conditioned response we desire (instant influence). Robert Cialdini, *Influence: The Psychology of Persuasion*, Revised Ed. Collins, New York, 1998.

[15] For more ideas on how to use musical vocabulary in your reading, see: http://www.music.vt.edu/musicdictionary/appendix/tempo/tempo3.html

[16] For a list of social book marking software, see: http://www.blogmarketingtactics.com/social-bookmarking/social-bookmarking-top-links.html

[17] Speed reading resources: check your speed http://www.readingsoft.com/ and http://www.ababasoft.com/speedreading/articles.html

[18] For more on these mindsets and their effect on interviews:, see Trond Arne Undheim, "Getting connected: how sociologists can access the high tech elite", *The Qualitative Report*, Volume 8, Number 1, June 2003, 104-128, http://www.nova.edu/ssss/QR/QR8-1/undheim.pdf The article includes comprehensive, academic references to the field of interview methods.

[19] The meeting quality program at Xerox Corporation is mentioned by Thomas H. Davenport in *Thinking for a living*, Harvard Business School Press, Boston, 2005, p. 113.

[20] All groups tend to have both task and maintenance dimensions. *Group Processes: dynamics within and between groups*, Rupert Brown, Oxford: Blackwell, 1988; *Small group decision making* (2nd ed), Fischer, B.A., New York: McGraw-Hill, 1980; *Intervention skills: Process consultation for small groups and teams*, Reddy, W.B., Johannesburg: Pfeiffer, 1994.

[21] A special thanks to Professor Sue D. Pendell at Colorado State University, for her inspiring tutorial on "Working successfully in teams" at the eChallenges 2005 conference in Ljubljana, Slovenia, 20 October, 2005, from whom many of our points in this chapter are derived.

[22] Some examples of empirical studies of virtual teams in international firms are:

an international polymer film producer (http://www.virtualteamsresearch.org/vtedmondson&sole.pdf), a Telco (http://dsslab.sims.monash.edu/DSS2004/proceedings/pdf/25_Faniel_Majchrzak.pdf), 54 companies' experience with "Far flung teams"(http://www-rcf.usc.edu/~majchrza/), three high tech companies described in an EU R&D project about virtual teams (http://www.relier.org/docs/Lisbonne.pdf; http://www.relier.org/uk/index.php; http://www.relier.org/uk/publications.php), an NSF-study of Fortune 500 global teams (http://www.virtualteamsresearch.org/1) etc.

[23] The US had such a body in the 1970s, called the Office of Technology Assessment. Most European countries have such a body, and they all contribute to public debate through a variety of projects, working with experts and also with laypeople's assessments.

[24] For reference to these "mobile working models", see "Mobile and collaborative workplaces: an agenda for innovation", by Schaffers et al., in P. Cunningham and M. Cunningham (Eds.), IOS Press, 2005, p.1218.

[25] Body language in the workplace: http://www.warrenshepell.com/articles/hq_04spring.asp

[26] A quick overview of the debates around whether there are 9 or 21 senses is found in Wikipedia http://en.wikipedia.org/wiki/Senses (accessed 11 November 2005).

[27] The best description of the proximity sense is fictional. Trevanian equips his main character Nicholai Hel with a strong proximity sense in the cult classic Shibumi (1979).

[28] *Phenomenology of perception* (Merleau-Ponty, 1945).

[29] SacredWorldFoundation is located in Dehli, India, has 25 employees and is led by Ranjit Makkuni. See http://www.sacredworld.com/ (accessed 11 November 2005).

[30] The Crossing Project of the Sacred World Foundation: http://www.crossingproject.net/default.htm

[31] *Birds*, Peterson Field Guides, Houghton Mifflin, Boston, 2002.

[32] Whether the feeling of strength actually makes people stronger is debatable. See http://news.bbc.co.uk/2/hi/health/239970.stm

[33] See Leadership in China: Keeping Pace with a Growing Economy, http://www.ddiworld.com/pdf/ddi_leadershipinchina_rr.pdf and http://iis-db.stanford.edu/pubs/21276/HS_ResultsInChina.pdf

[34] Interview with CNN: http://edition.cnn.com/2007/WORLD/asiapcf/06/03/talkasia.cheungyan/index.html Also see: http://www.erim.eur.nl/ERIM/Research/Centres/China_Business/Featuring/Featuring%20Detail?p_item_id=5012025&p_pg_id=93&p_page_id=2286308

[35] See http://www.rediff.com/money/2007/may/28bspec.htm

[36] Narayana Murthy, see http://en.wikipedia.org/wiki/N._R._Narayana_Murthy

[37] Kibun (기분), meaning "pride", "face", "vitality", "life-force", "feeling," "mood,"or "state of mind" and Nunchi (눈치) are closely related. Kibun might be described as the part of you that goes beyond your physical presence, something that not only permeates your being but surrounds you, invisibly, like a cloud. Maintaining Kibun means doing what feels right and what will result in the most socially harmonious outcome for everyone involved, which is not to say that Koreans are not rational. You hurt someone's *kibun* by being argumentative, giving bad news, or ignoring Korean social rankings, but if you have high *kibun* you can do more without worry. Kibun is only one of the six controlling concepts of the Korean psyche: saving face (*chemyeon*), gauging another's mood (*neunchi*), mood (kibun), being convivial and maintaining group mood (*bunuiki*), loving attachment to one's closest circle (*jeong/cheong*) and sorrow and rage towards injustice, often manifested in bad vibes (*han*), which makes Korea a high context culture, Nunchi refers to a concept in Korean culture, described as "the subtle art of listening and gauging another's mood". Koreans are taught not to make their true feelings shown so generally others have to use nunchi to guess how the other is feeling (one could maybe apply the English expression 'poker face' to convey a similar idea). Nunchi is literally translated as "eye-measure". However, regarding other issues, such as bodily appearance, Koreans can be surprisingly frank. See http://ask.metafilter.com/10490/

[38] See http://www.strategy-business.com/li/leadingideas/li00020

[39] Kaizen (改善), Japanese for "change for the better" or "improvement"; the common English usage is "continuous improvement", where kai (改) means 'change' and Zen (善) means 'good'.. In the Japanese context as applied to Toyota employee practices it means continuous improvement in the personal life, home life, social life and working life, achieved by eliminating wasteful practices one by one and standardizing new practices. See http://en.wikipedia.org/wiki/Kaizen

[40] Genchi Genbutsu (現地現物) means "go and see for yourself" and it is an integral part of the Toyota Production System, see: http://en.wikipedia.org/wiki/Genchi_Genbutsu , a related concept is the Gemba attitude (see http://en.wikipedia.org/wiki/Gemba) Gemba being a Japanese term meaning "the place where the truth can be found". In Toyota's manufacturing practice, it means that if a problem occurs, the engineers must go there to understand the full impact of the problem, gathering data from all sources, and must not solely rely on witness account, trying to address the issue remotely.

[41] Nemawashi (根回し) in Japanese culture is an informal process of quietly laying the foundation for some proposed change or project, by talking to the people concerned, gathering support and feedback, and so forth, and literally translates as "going around the roots", from 根 (ne, root) and 回す (mawasu, to go around [something]), see http://en.wikipedia.org/wiki/Nemawashi

[42] For more background on Toyota, see http://en.wikipedia.org/wiki/The_Toyota_Way, http://en.wikipedia.org/wiki/Toyota and http://www.amazon.com/How-Toyota-Became-Leadership-Greatest/dp/1591841798

[43] See http://en.wikipedia.org/wiki/Fuyo_Group

[44] A keiretsu (系列, literally meaning system or series, is a set of companies with interlocking business relationships and shareholdings, see http://en.wikipedia.org/wiki/Keiretsu

[45] For more insight on Carlos Ghosn, see http://en.wikipedia.org/wiki/Carlos_Ghosn and http://www.amazon.com/exec/obidos/ASIN/0071248676/garreynoldsc-20/002-

3582192-9819255?%5Fencoding=UTF8&camp=1789&link%5Fcode=xm2,
http://www.strategy-business.com/press/16635507/11268,
http://www.managementtoday.co.uk/search/article/549439/carlos-ghosn-leadership-starts-transparency/ and
http://www.icmrindia.org/casestudies/catalogue/Leadership%20and%20Entrepreneurship/LDEN020.htm

46 On Sony, see http://en.wikipedia.org/wiki/Sony and
http://www.informationarbitrage.com/2007/03/howard_stringer.html

47 Weber, 1922; 1947; 1968.

48 See:
http://www.elsevier.com/wps/find/bookdescription.cws_home/637430/description#description

49 Bruno Latour, *Reassembling the Social: An Introduction to Actor-Network-Theory*, Oxford University Press, 2005.

50 On Feng shui, see http://en.wikipedia.org/wiki/Feng_shui or Gill Hale, The Practical Encyclopedia of Feng Shui, Hermes House, London, 2005.

51 John Bowlby, *The making and breaking of affectional bonds,* London, Routledge, 1990 [1977].

52 See Oldenburg's book on the topic of loss of social place,
http://en.wikipedia.org/wiki/Ray_Oldenburg

53 http://inventors.about.com/library/inventors/blpostit.htm and
http://en.wikipedia.org/wiki/Post-it_note Incidentally, one of the authors also uses sticky notes to organize his own hymnals. In fact, they were used with success during a Christmas Concert in 2006.

54 Rapid Problem Solving with Post-It Notes, by David Straker, 1997, Gower Publishing, Aldershot, Hampshire, Great Britain.

55 "Telenor's new headquarters to open on September 23", Telenor press release 22 September 2002: http://press.telenor.com/PR/200209/874437_5.html

56 Danish e-invoicing best practice case, epractice.eu:
http://www.epractice.eu/cases/1967

57 http://europa.eu.int/idabc/en/document/4215/194

58 Geert Hofstede's website: http://www.geert-hofstede.com/

59 World Values Surveys: http://wvs.isr.umich.edu/

60 http://www.ethnologue.com/

61 http://www.timesonline.co.uk/article/0,,2095-2281123.html

62 Marianne Gullestad, "The Scandinavian version of Egalitarian Individualism",
http://etnhum.etn.lu.se/eth_scand/text/1991/1991_3-18.PDF

63 "The Nordic Model: A recipe for European success?", *EPC Working Paper No.20*, September 2005. http://www.theepc.be/

64 See http://www.spiegel.de/international/spiegel/0,1518,465438,00.html

65 http://www.mc.maricopa.edu/dept/d10/asb/anthro2003/glues/leadership.html

66 Al Qaeda: http://en.wikipedia.org/wiki/Al_Quaida

67 Bengt Gustavsson, "The Human Values of Swedish Management", *Journal of Human Values* (Sage Press, New Delhi), vol.1, no 2, 1995, pp 153-172. http://www.fek.su.se/Home/gus/PAPERS/Swedval.htm

68 Finding The Balance: Pernille Spiers-Lopez, Miriam Marcus, Forbes, 03.19.07, see http://www.forbes.com/2007/03/19/spiers-lopez-balance-lead-careers-worklife07-cx_mlm_0319spierslopez.html

69 IKEA:
http://www.ikea.com/ms/en_US/about_ikea/facts_figures/ikea_in_the_world.html;
http://knowledge.wharton.upenn.edu/article/959.cfm;
http://en.wikipedia.org/wiki/Ikea;
http://www.businessweek.com/magazine/content/05_46/b3959001.htm;
http://www.workforce.com/section/09/feature/23/79/57/index.html

70 McKinsey case
http://www.mckinsey.com/aboutus/whatwedo/workexamples/leadership_priority.asp

71 Haldor Byrkjeflot et al, *The Democratic Challenge to Capitalism*, Fagbokforlaget, Bergen, Norway, 1991.

72 Mr Kjell Inge Røkke's speech at Maritime Industries Forum Plenary Session

in Oslo, Norway, 5 October 2006:
http://64.233.169.104/search?q=cache:IXgpJ92fO6sJ:www.maritimt-forum.no/default.asp%3FFILE%3Ditems/2164/230/0610%2520KIR%2520Opening%2520speech%2520MIF%2520Oslo.pdf+Kjell+Inge+R%C3%B8kke+leader&hl=en&ct=clnk&cd=4&gl=us&client=firefox-a (my translation).

73 http://www.internetworldstats.com/stats.htm

74 http://www.gartner.com/press_releases/asset_146385_11.html

75 Wikipedia: http://en.wikipedia.org/wiki/Main_Page

76 http://en.wikipedia.org/wiki/Semantic_Web

77 See Julius Fast, *Body Language*, New York, Simon & Schuster, 1970 and Stephan Schiffman, *Cold Calling Techniques*, Adams Media Corporation, 2003.

78 On presentation software, see: http://en.wikipedia.org/wiki/Presentation_program

79 On the history of the slide projector, see: http://en.wikipedia.org/wiki/Slide_projector

80 On the history of the overhead projector, see:
http://en.wikipedia.org/wiki/Overhead_projector

81 On the history of Power Point, see:
http://www.maniactive.com/states/2005/10/powerpoint-backgroundliterally.html; Ian Parker's New Yorker article *Absolute PowerPoint*, May 20, 2001, pp. 76-87. http://rneedsu.rutgers.edu/BPW/BPW/BReadings/Absolute_PowerPoint.pdf and http://www.physics.ohio-state.edu/~wilkins/group/powerpt.html. Another piece of PowerPoint scholarship is David K. Farkas' article "Understanding and Using PowerPoint," STC Annual Conference Proceedings, May 8-11, 2005, pp. 313-320 (http://faculty.washington.edu/farkas/TC510/Farkas-STC-05-UnderstandingPowerPoint.pdf).

82 For examples of the anti-Power Point movement, see: PowerPoint Antidote, by Peter Norvig (2000) where he has made a mock-up PowerPoint version of the Gettysburg address: http://norvig.com/Gettysburg/ and http://cimc.education.wisc.edu/help_instruction/instruc_materials/ppessay.htm

83 Edward D. Tufte, *The Cognitive Style of PowerPoint*: http://www.edwardtufte.com/tufte/

84 For more on presentation zen, see http://www.presentationzen.com/presentationzen/

85 About Open Office and Impress, see: http://en.wikipedia.org/wiki/OpenOffice.org#Components

86 For additional advice on presentation skills and Power Point, see: http://www.indezine.com/articles/goldentriangle.html, this example of bad practice: http://cit.information.unl.edu/tips/Webpage/saveasjpegs/index.shtmland; and Microsoft's own advice: http://office.microsoft.com/en-us/FX010857971033.aspx

87 On the history of digital projectors, see: http://en.wikipedia.org/wiki/Digital_projector

88 See http://www.blogherald.com/

89 See Harriet Zuckerman, *Scientific Elite: Nobel Laureates in the United States*, Transaction Publishers, 1996.

90 See p.26 http://www.cda-acd.forces.gc.ca/CFLI/engraph/research/pdf/75.pdf (19.11.05).

91 http://www.lancs.ac.uk/fss/sociology/papers/hughes-et-al-problems-of-organisation.pdf

92 See http://en.wikipedia.org/wiki/Zone_of_proximal_development

93 See p.26: http://www.cda-acd.forces.gc.ca/CFLI/engraph/research/pdf/75.pdf

94 http://www.nwlink.com/~donclark/hrd/learning/styles.html#kolb

95 John W. Kingdon, *Agendas, Alternatives and Public Policies*, 2nd edition, Harper Collins, New York, 1995 [1984].

96 In writing up this case study, we have read lots of material on company culture, programming, and/or Open Source. Notably, Deal, T. & Kennedy, A. (1988) *Corporate Cultures*. Harmondsworth: Penguin; Kunda, G. (1992). *Engineering culture: Control and commitment in a high-tech corporation*. Philadelphia: Temple University Press; Lakhani, Karen R., Wolf, B. & Bates, J. (2002) "The Boston Consulting Group Hacker survey", release 0.3, GNU free document license v.1.1. www.bcg.com/opensource; Weinberg, Gerald M. (1971) *The psychology of computer programming*. New York: Dorset.

97 The name of the company and individual employees has been changed to maintain anonymity.

98 Tom Demarco and Timothy Lister, *Peopleware*, Dorset House Publishing Company, Incorporated; 2nd edition (February 1, 1999).

99 Geoffrey A. Moore, *Crossing the Chasm: marketing and selling high tech products to mainstream customers* , Harper Collins, New York, 1991.

100 Donald A. Norman, *The design of everyday things*, New York, Basic Books, 2002 [1988].

101 Frederick P. Brooks Jr., *The mythical man-month*, Addison Wesley, 1995 [1975].

102 Extreme Programming: http://www.extremeprogramming.org/rules.html